THE PROVERBS' GUIDE TO LOVE

Third Edition

Written by Armand J. Azamar

Foreword by Jay Peters

Broken Owl Productions™

Copyright © 2011 by Armand J. Azamar

All rights reserved. No part of this publication may be reproduced, stored in a retrieval system, or transmitted in any form or by any means – electronic, mechanical, photocopy, recording, scanning, or other – except for brief quotations in critical reviews or articles, without the prior written permission of the publisher.

Scripture quotations are taken from the Holy Bible: New King James Version © 1982 by Thomas Nelson, Inc. Used by Permission. All rights reserved.

Cover art by Armand J. Azamar

Published by Broken Owl Productions™, Glenwood, IL

If you are interested in purchasing more print copies, or even an e-book version, please visit www.thebrokenowl.com.

Created in the United States of America

ISBN-10: 0984902937

ISBN-13: 978-0-9849029-3-4

Purchase more print copies or the Kindle version here:

Follow the author on Instagram here:

Listen to sermons from New Life Assembly Church here:

Table of Contents

Foreword 5

Chapter 1 – Let's Start 7

Chapter 2 – Flirt to Convert 11

Chapter 3 – Areas of Grey 21

Chapter 4 – Infatuation 31

Chapter 5 – Lust 47

Chapter 6 – Samson and Solomon 56

Chapter 7 – Porn 63

Chapter 8 – Singlehood 76

Chapter 9 – Dating 89

Chapter 10 – Waiting 100

Chapter 11 – Advice from the Married 111

Chapter 12 – A Lack of Commitment 125

Chapter 13 – Proverbs' Guide to Love 135

Chapter 14 – God is Love 149

Chapter 15 – Conclusion 163

References 168

About the Author 173

Foreword

My friendship with Armand goes back about 10 years ago, when he began to attend my youth group. Over the years, I have seen continued growth and progression in his walk with Christ. I can attest to his commitment as a young single to following the principles of this book. Over time, Armand has matured and become a vital part of our ministry, both in teaching and preaching the word of God. More importantly his talk meets his walk; which is a rare commodity these days.

After reading the final draft of *The Proverbs' Guide to Love,* my first thought was, "I need to tell every young adult serving Christ to read this book." My second thought was to ask Armand if I could write the foreword. I am confident God will use this book to strengthen Christians to pursue relationships His way and not the broken system of the world.

Being in ministry for over 20 years, I have seen the devastating effect of relationships and marriages that are not anchored in the person of Jesus Christ. What I deeply appreciate about Armand's approach is his commitment to biblical accuracy and forthrightness in declaring the straight way of the Lord in a crooked and perverse generation. Much of what he writes runs polar opposite to our culture and sadly the majority of the Church. Yet, it is these truths the people of God so desperately need to experience true love and freedom.

Over the years, I have read several books on this topic. Many were helpful. However, in *Proverbs' Guide*, two thoughts come to mind: thorough and practical. If you are a young Christian and desire to have a greater understanding in relationships, I believe you will find solid biblical counsel and expert advice that will allow you to glorify God and build a marriage that will last a lifetime.

- Jay Peters, Associate Pastor of New Life Assembly Church (www.nlachurch.com), January 2012

Chapter 1 – Let's Start

Our church has a men's meeting every third Saturday of the month. I get up at about 6:30 am in the morning, since it starts at 7 am. The meeting consists of younger believers as well as veteran believers and is a very loose format. Discussion is encouraged, and almost anyone is allowed to speak.

This time, the men's group leader asked David to speak. That Saturday morning, David gave us the title of his message: *Fifty Steps to a Successful Marriage*. Normally, this wouldn't be a shocking message. However, this message title proved to be a bit troubling, seeing how David was only married for a year!

I remember my Pastor placing his face in his hands. I could not tell if it was in amusement or disappointment. Three of the men sitting there had been married for at least twenty years. Even I felt David's message was going to end in humiliation.

David explained that the message title was a trick; it was a setup for his real message. The true title of David's message was *God's Credibility*. David threw out the *Fifty Steps* as an example of his own lack of credibility. In other words, when a Christian speaks on a certain topic, they need credibility. David noted that it would be illogical for him to speak about marriage since he himself was only married for a year.

Even though David lacked credibility, this book's subject matter isn't a setup. *The Proverbs' Guide to Love* is about love, lust, marriage, dating and divorce.

Where do I, a 24-year-old single man, come off talking about such controversial things? At least David was married for a year! In reality, this *Guide* contains my seeking out advice from married couples. I didn't interview couples that have been married for just a few years. I interviewed couples that have been married for at least ten years; I interviewed those that are credible. I must note that not all interviews are incorporated here; however, it forms the basis of this *Guide*.

I am a college student. I am studying for my Bachelors in Communications, with a concentration in Journalism. So, I may not know what it is like to be married; nevertheless, I try to ask the right questions to those that are married.

I started to take interest in relationships within the Church around 2005. I attended a college-level church group several years ago, when I was about 18 years old. In my dealings with Christian peers, I began to notice a strange predicament. This problem took the form of missionary dating.

Missionary dating is the act of a Christian dating a nonbeliever, with the intention or hope of saving the nonbeliever. It concerned me. I began to notice a trend within my youth group that resulted in destructive relationships.

I remember addressing one of my friends who got involved in missionary dating.

"Well," I said. "You know what is coming, right?"

"Yes." My Christian friend told me plainly that they were dating a lost person.

I reminded my friend that what they were doing was against the Bible. I still remember the response: "I don't care what the Bible says; I am going to do what I want."

Although blatant, at least my friend was honest. A lot of times, people try and justify themselves or find loopholes in the Bible. I must at least give my friend credit for being sincere.

Friends need to help other friends if they are going in the wrong direction (Proverbs 27:5,6). This is especially needed in the body of Christ. I attempted to warn a few of my close Christian friends of getting involved in missionary dating. However, my warnings were only meet with derision.

The defiance wasn't against me. The defiance is against the Word of God. Someone who is not a Christian may not understand the purpose of this book. But, to someone who is a believer, one might be able to understand my dire concern for my fellow Christians.

The missionary dating of my peers tempted me. For a moment, I thought, "Why in the world am I waiting for the Lord to send me a

Christian mate? My brothers and sisters in Christ aren't waiting for the Lord."

Thus, the *Guide* was born.

So, I sought out advice on marriage, originally gathering the notes as an aid for myself. However, it occurred to me that I wanted to share my findings with others. Also, I did not write this book as an expert. I wrote this book as someone who is exploring the dynamics of relationships within the Church.

Missionary dating is the starting point, and my notes from married couples form the foundation. However, as mentioned, dating, singlehood, divorce, lust, and love will be addressed.

Hopefully, this book will be a blessing to others.

Chapter 2 – Flirt to Convert

Missionary dating is the act of a Christian dating a lost person with the intention or hope of seeing the lost person saved. Sometimes, it is used to rationalize a romantic interest in a nonbeliever. Intention or hope of salvation doesn't necessarily need to be stated, as it is somewhat implied. So, the simplest definition of missionary dating is a Christian dating a lost person. Clearly, Scripture is against this.

2 Corinthians 6:14-16 says,

14. Do not be unequally yoked together with unbelievers. For what fellowship has righteousness with lawlessness? And what communion has light with darkness? 15. And what accord has Christ with Belial? Or what part has a believer with an unbeliever? 16. And what agreement has the temple of God with idols? For you are the temple of the living God. As God has said: "I will dwell in them and walk among [them]. I will be their God, and they shall be My people."

What communion does light have with darkness? Paul asked a rhetorical question. They don't mix. No matter how hard you try and mix light and darkness, they simply can't mix.

Verse 14 mentions being *yoked together with unbelievers*. A yoke is a U-shaped frame fitted over the necks of labor animals, particularly oxen. The two animals move in the same direction. This gives the impression of two working together.

I am not saying that a believer should join with any person who calls him or herself a Christian. I am not saying to date someone just because they go to church. We need to seek out a Christian who shows the fruits of salvation (Matthew 7:16-20). In other words, we need someone who visibly has Jesus as Lord, rather than someone who simply calls Jesus Lord.

If unbelievers are yoked with believers, the yoke will be uneven. I must note, this doesn't include instances where a person in an unbelieving married couple becomes a believer. The image of an unbeliever and believer being yoked together implies disorder; they will be going in opposite directions. Amos 3:3 says, c*an two walk together, unless they are agreed?*

Interview: Date to Save

During the course of writing this book, I came across many ministries that were very helpful. First and foremost was *Date to Save*. Some have taken the ministry seriously; however, it is simply a good parody of where the modern Church is.

A Christian under the guise of "Tamara" runs *Date to Save* (now defunct). She created the webpage to inform and help believers on their missionary dating ventures. Tamara says that Christian women should use their beauty for Christ, in fulfillment of the Great Commission.

The content of *Date to Save* (datetosave.com) is very exaggerated. Even so, it did get a few people fooled. I even came across a Baptist podcast that condemns the actions of the website.

In addition, I asked the ministry if they were real or not on Twitter. Their response was, "No, it's just good ol' fashion satire!"

Tamara goes on to explain the logic of missionary dating on the homepage, stating that our bodies are a living sacrifice. The *Questions* page offers help for lovesick Christians. One critic asks if God looks down on missionary dating and references being *unequally yoked* from 2 Corinthians 6:14. Here's Tamara's response:

I looked up yoked, and the dictionary says it's "A crossbar with two U-shaped pieces that encircles the necks of a pair of oxen..." I would never encourage anybody to do this on a date...I think the thing that is more important is that we use our talents for God. If you're really good at dating, or just really good looking, then you should use that to bring souls to God.

These exaggerations reflect a real attitude. In something as nonsensical as missionary dating, how can you not get a bit silly?

I got a chance to interview Tamara about *Date to Save*, minus the parody guise. She stated that missionary dating has always been a running joke within the evangelical community, as well as a source of judgment. Tamara believes very few Christians purposefully date for the sake of the Great Commission. Yet, the thought of taking the concept, and making it into a full-blown ministry was funny.

"I became a Christian in late high school, so naturally, I learned of the term fairly quickly in my church's youth group." Tamara said.

Tamara receives a wide array of responses for *Date to Save*. These responses usually fall within one of two categories: an understanding of the joke versus legitimate concern. Legitimate concern is then divided into two subcategories: concerns from believers and concerns from nonbelievers. Both concerns are similar, as both sides understand the general negativity of someone getting into a relationship with an ulterior motive.

Tamara notes an occasional third type of response: one of praise. Tamara even quoted a recent message to her, which stated, "I'd like to say that it's very cool that you want to bring souls to Christ!" Even Tamara herself is confused by such e-mails. She said that these kind of e-mails almost always get responses from her, since she doesn't really want people to mistake subtle satire for a valid way to live out their faith.

"I can honestly say that I have seen it work out, where someone came to know Christ through dating a believer," Tamara said. "But, if you're interested in playing odds, I think they're better in Vegas."

I must also note that in my interviews with ministry folk, some have remembered rare instances where the unbeliever eventually got saved. However, I also noticed in my research that this outcome isn't always picture perfect (as will be discussed in the next chapter).

Tamara has been married for close to a decade. When I asked her why Christians justify missionary dating, she said that rationalization for sin is universal to both believers and nonbelievers. She noted James 4, which shows internal passions and desires to be the source of our sin.

Tamara doesn't believe that every aspect of missionary dating is sin (I differ, in that I see missionary dating as more of a symptom of a compromised heart). Since some of the same internal passions ring true today, Christians can still succumb to worldly temptations. Dating, or more generally, wanting to be with someone, can be usurped and turned into ungodly desire.

"Desires for someone of a different or no faith, more often than not leads to some rationalization that good might come of it," Tamara said. "Including misusing verse like *all things work together for good to them that love God* (Romans 8:28), forgetting that obedience is a fruit of that love for God."

Oil and Water

Have you ever tried mixing oil and water? Remember those science experiments back in elementary school? First, you get some water and some oil. Then, you put it in a glass cup and you get a spoon. Next, you try your best to mix the oil and the water.

After swishing it around for a while, it may look like a combined mixture. But it doesn't take long for the water and the oil to separate. No matter how hard you would try, the oil and water cannot mix perfectly, because they are two completely different substances.

Like in our little science experiment, the lost and the saved cannot mix perfectly because they are two different substances. To be more specific, they are of two different parentages. 1 Thessalonians 5:5 says, *you are all sons of light and sons of the day. We are not of the night nor of darkness.*

The missionary dater thinks they know better than God. Though the missionary dater will try to find a way to make the oil and water of their relationships mix. However, Proverbs 14:12 says, *there is a way [that seems] right to a man, but its end [is] the way of death.*

Many explanations and excuses can be used in the pursuit of the lost love interest. They are cute. They go to church, a little. They will accept Jesus as their Savior, eventually.

I heard Christian girls saying bizarre things to put their boyfriends in the right light. "Oh, well, he is not *that* Christian," or "He knows about God, but he doesn't know what to do with it."

Remember the rhetorical question Paul asks in 2 Corinthians 6:14: *what communion does light have with darkness?* The Christian was once of darkness, being lost. But now, they are of the light

(Ephesians 5:8). Likewise, Paul places a clear difference between believers and nonbelievers.

To the world, we are supposed to be a light (Matthew 5:14). The light can make the lost uncomfortable, because it reveals their sin (John 3:19-21). In reality, believers are meant to be little versions of the Light, Jesus Christ (John 1).

It may seem like light and darkness can mix, for a while. Even oil and water look like they can mix for a while. But, time, trials and tribulation will show the union as imperfect. And that imperfection may show itself as blatant as a divorce or as subtle as a flawed thinking pattern. In the end, God Himself will completely separate the saved from the lost (Matthew 25:31-46).

But what if the darkness becomes light? What if the lost does accept Christ through missionary dating? That will be discussed in the next chapter.

One Flesh, One Spirit

The flippant attitude we take with dating (and even marriage) is another basis for missionary dating. We do not take relationships seriously. Oftentimes, relationships are self-serving. Relationships are made and broken with little regard as to what Jesus desires.

In 1 Corinthians 6:14-17, Paul describes a Corinth Christian who joins with a harlot. It says,

14. And God both raised up the Lord and will also raise us up by His power. 15. Do you not know that your bodies are members of Christ? Shall I then take the members of Christ and make [them] members of a harlot? Certainly not! 16. Or do you not know that he who is joined to a harlot is one body [with her]? For "the two," He says, "shall become one flesh." 17. But he who is joined to the Lord is one spirit [with Him].

Verse 16 references Genesis 2:22-24, where the Lord institutes marriage as being between a man and a woman. Man and woman will become one. So they will share in each other's weaknesses, strengths, and thoughts. Their lives will become one.

The Christian addressed by Paul disregarded the sacredness of marriage. He had no idea that his body was part of the members of Jesus Christ. Many of us today lack the same understanding.

As Christians, we are the body of Christ (1 Corinthians 12:27). Our bodies are a living sacrifice (Romans 12:1) and the temple of the Holy Spirit (1 Corinthians 6:19). How thoughtless would it be then to join this body with a harlot? How foolish would it be to join Christ's body with a promiscuous woman, who joins herself with many men?

I doubt many Christians will join themselves to a prostitute. That is obviously wrong; however, many Christians join themselves with an unbeliever. And the end result of such unions often leads to disaster. This does not mean we shouldn't have lost friends.

Nevertheless, just like the children of Israel, joining to a nonbeliever in marriage may cause us to chase after "other gods" (Deuteronomy 30:17).

1 Corinthians 5:6 says, *a little leaven leavens the whole lump.* The compromised Christian may think they are only giving a small foothold or an insignificant part of their life. Unexpectedly, that small bit can infect the believer's entire spiritual walk. The believer may not even realize it before it is too late. This is even more important when forming serious relationships (such as dating and marriage).

Why did Paul write 1 Corinthians 6? If we read on, we see the Corinthian church had problems with sexual sins. The letter reminds them that their salvation didn't come cheap.

1 Corinthians 6:18-20 says,

18. Flee sexual immorality. Every sin that a man does is outside the body, but he who commits sexual immorality sins against his own body. 19. Or do you not know that your body is the temple of the Holy Spirit [who is] in you, whom you have from God, and you are not your own? 20. For you were bought at a price; therefore glorify God in your body and in your spirit, which are God's.

The Christian is bought with a price. That price is the blood of Jesus Christ (Colossians 1:20). By the blood of Christ, we are justified and saved from wrath (Romans 5:9). We do not own ourselves. The body and spirit belong to God.

There will always be a spiritual conflict between believers and the world, until Jesus Christ comes back (John 15:18-20). Missionary dating is only a glimpse of how the modern Church compromises its purity in order to satisfy its desire.

If the Christian is willing to compromise their relationship with God for a relationship with an unbeliever, what else are they willing to compromise?

Chapter 3 – Areas of Grey

Throughout the Old Testament, God warns the children of Israel to not marry those of the heathen nations. Examples of this include Joshua 23:7 and Nehemiah 10:30. This warning wasn't based on race or ethnicity. After all, there are several instances of Gentiles assimilating into Israel in the Old Testament. Ruth stands as the most prominent example. Instead, this warning is based on gods the person worshipped.

Marriage to the heathens would turn the heart of Israel away from God (Deuteronomy 7:2-4). Ezra 9 gives an example of Israel disobeying God's warning. A complaint is brought to the scribe.

Ezra 9:1,2 says,

1. When these things were done, the leaders came to me, saying, "The people of Israel and the priests and the Levites have not separated themselves from the peoples of the lands, with respect to the abominations of the Canaanites, the Hittites, the Perizzites, the Jebusites, the Ammonites, the Moabites, the Egyptians, and the Amorites. 2. For they have taken some of their daughters as wives for themselves and their sons, so that the holy seed is mixed with the peoples of those lands. Indeed, the hand of the leaders and rulers has been foremost in this trespass."

When Ezra heard of this, he rent his clothes (Ezra 9:3). It wasn't just the people who integrated with the heathen nations; the leaders were chief in this trespass.

Likewise, many modern Christians may cite leaders in their church who successfully missionary dated. Young Christians may say, "If it worked out for them, it will work out for me."

The incident in Ezra didn't end too well. The house of God confessed their sin (Ezra 10:1). Then, they put away their pagan wives as well as those born of them (Ezra 10:2,3). When believers (especially Christian leaders) choose to join with unbelievers, there is a cost. Of special note, the separation in Ezra was most likely done to preserve the Messianic lineage. Today, God does not permit separation (such as divorce) if missionary dating does not succeed.

Young Christians watch leaders like this. They reference them, as several have done. As stated before, "If it worked out for them, it may work out for me," is the common phrase I have heard. However, success doesn't make a wrong right.

We must not confuse God's mercy with God's perfect will. We must look at the bigger picture.

Justification For

Down throughout the years, I have seen many justifications for missionary dating. One of the justifications I heard was that God expects us to do some work. Another justification is that God expects people in our lives for a reason. Some advice by church leaders is to get the lost person in a group with other Christians. Still other believers also advise babies in Christ to spiritually grow before endeavoring to missionary date. Unlike the satire of *Date to Save*, these justifications and tips made by church leaders are very real.

If a Christian is open and admits they are backslidden, I (as a church teacher) would be much more understanding. In other words, if a backslider missionary dates, it is irrelevant. If a believer is honest, there is more room for healing when the Christian desires restoration. However, when a believer tries to justify their self-will, healing is hindered.

Chuck Smith, Pastor of Calvary Chapel Costa Mesa stated that many Christians believe themselves to be the exception. Christians believe, especially young adults, that they will be successful.

"You cannot go against the word of God and win," Smith said. "Over the years of pastoring, I've had so many young people come in. Oh, they are so in love. Oh, he's the man of their dreams."

The only problem would be that he wouldn't be a believer. Smith noted how the woman would typically say that she could win him, if she walks in humility and love. Smith would bring up the Scripture, only to be shot down by the surety of the lost companion's future salvation.

They marry. And years down the road, Pastor Smith would sit

down with the same broken young woman.

""Oh, I wish I had listened to you. I'm living in a hell. I don't think I ever really loved him. Oh, this is horrible. Do I have to stay in this state?" And their lives [are] messed up because they thought that they could go against God's command and win and come out ahead," Smith said.

2 Corinthians 6:14-16 has deeper applications than just an unbeliever being yoked with a believer. This can also include two opposing callings.

For example, let's say that a Christian man and a Christian woman meet each other. Both are completely devoted to God; however, one is called to the mission field in Africa. The other is called to the inner city of Chicago. Both have two different calls, and thus both have two different yokes.

Most Christians will not think twice about a relationship, especially if that potential mate shows the slightest sign of faith. Moreover, what God calls us to must be considered as well. We must pray for someone who will help us in the yoke God has given us.

Three Things to Consider

Here are three things to consider regarding missionary dating.

First, only God the Father can draw men. John 6:44 says, *no man can come to me unless the Father who sent Me draws him; and I will raise him up at the last day.*

Missionary dating is an attempt to draw an unbeliever in order to fulfill a desire for a relationship. The unbeliever is not coming to Christ for salvation; the unbeliever is coming to Christ for a relationship. Only the Father can draw men (John 6:44), not the flirtations of a believer. The Holy Spirit convicts sinners (John 16:8). The Cross of Jesus reconciles sinners to God (Ephesians 2:16).

All of this begs the question: is someone who is saved through missionary dating actually saved? It is possible. God uses flawed methods all the time. Nonetheless, this is not meant to promote the flawed methods.

Missionary dating does bring salvation into question. And it doesn't just bring the question into the mind of watchers. But, it also brings the question into the mind of the missionary dater. In other words, why did this person really accept Christ?

Second, missionary dating is really a symptom of the heart. Again, 2 Corinthians 6:14 says, *what communion has light with darkness?* Missionary dating is more like a symptom of a backslidden heart, instead of a cause. If the Christian desires to join with an unbeliever, then the heart is already having issues with the lordship of Jesus Christ.

Verse 14 is not speaking of unbelievers who are just friends, or acquaintances. For example, Jesus Himself was a friend of sinners (Matthew 11:19). Instead, the verse talks about deeper fellowship, such as dating and marriages. This also includes business relationships.

If the believer does have communion with darkness, then the heart must hunger for darkness. Our soul should thirst for God, not for the affection of an unbeliever (Psalms 42:2).

Third, missionary dating is deceitful to the unbeliever. Leviticus 19:11 says, *you shall not steal, nor deal falsely, nor lie to one another.*

"It is a little humorous (and sad at the same time), that some believers don't pick up or focus on the manipulative nature of true missionary dating and the potential consequences for the non-Christian, but solely focus on the personal holiness of the individual Christian and how Scripture is being misinterpreted," said Tamara of *Date to Save*. "Really, all should be concerns. But it's weird how some people don't think of the unbeliever in all of this."

Missionary dating shows that the believer's love was conditional. In other words, it is a love based on what the believer wants the unbeliever to be. One atheist blogger (after being the victim of missionary dating) called it cruel, unloving, self-serving and extremely disrespectful. This deceitful act can leave a bad taste in the mouth of the unbeliever.

"I have [believing] friends that dated people that don't have a faith rooted in Christ, and more often than not, it left a weird view of

Christianity for the non-Christians," said Tamara.

Blatant vs. Subtle

When missionary dating is addressed in the Church, the blatant effects are normally brought up. These include the believer backsliding, dropping out of church, mixed messages to children, and divorce. Some even note the unbeliever getting the believer involved in pornography and alcohol.

These are all reasonable concerns. But what is even worse than any of these blatant effects is if missionary dating actually "works out" and what "working out" does to the Christian's thinking.

I managed to interview a Christian couple where missionary dating was "successful"; the husband did become a believer. When I asked the wife about missionary dating in light of Scripture, she responded, "As I get older, I see that there are a lot more grey areas [in terms of right and wrong] in the Bible."

I didn't catch it at first, but I began thinking about it. Did this wife really find more grey areas in the Bible as she got older? Or did she simply learn how to jump over Scriptural barriers and sear her conscience? 1 Timothy 4:2 says, *having their own conscience seared with a hot iron.* Note the "own" refers to a self-deception.

The inability to discern correctly is worse than the blatant, disastrous effects. It is much more subtle and thus more hazardous. At least if things fall apart, the need to repent is evident.

Let's take missionary dating for example. If the lost mate leaves, the greatest lost the Christian receives is a broken heart. The break-up was the end of something that God did not ordain to begin with. In the end, the believer must allow the Lord to heal the broken heart.

Hebrews 12:5-11 says,

5. And you have forgotten the exhortation which speaks to you as to sons: "My son, do not despise the chastening of the Lord, nor be discouraged when you are rebuked by Him; 6. For whom the Lord loves He chastens, and scourges every son whom He receives." 7. If you endure chastening, God deals with you as with sons; for what son is there whom a father does not chasten? 8. But if you are without chastening, of which all have become partakers, then you are illegitimate and not sons. 9. Furthermore, we have had human fathers who corrected [us], and we paid [them] respect. Shall we not much more readily be in subjection to the Father of spirits and live? 10. For they indeed for a few days chastened [us] as seemed [best] to them, but He for [our] profit, that [we] may be partakers of His holiness. 11. Now no chastening seems to be joyful for the present, but painful; nevertheless, afterward it yields the peaceable fruit of righteousness to those who have been trained by it.

God's chastening is His mercy. It shows that God still loves the Christian as a Father. It shows that God is unwilling to let the Christian continue in rebellion. Praise God that He restricts us when we need it.

What if God doesn't chasten and permits compromise to continue unhindered? That's when the Christian needs to be concerned. Honestly, can the believer go against God's will and not be burned? Proverbs 6:23-29 asks a similar question. Whether blatant or subtle, the rebellious Christian will be burned.

There's something bad that happens when we disobey God and we think we got away with it. You might start thinking something is grey when it is actually black and white.

I have been tempted to missionary date several times. Personally, I think it is a common temptation that many young believers will face. However, several things blocked my pursuit. First, I don't want to be a hypocrite, especially after writing this book. Second, I don't want compromise, as missionary dating can make all my work for God's kingdom up until that point somewhat hollow. Third, I didn't want to manipulate the woman into a dishonest relationship.

Tamara said that we need to be honest with ourselves as to why we are attracted to certain people, knowing that our human side doesn't play favorites between believer and nonbeliever when it comes to looks and personality.

"We can't over-spiritualize attraction," she said. "We, nonetheless, must try our best to live within the bounds of the covenant that God has made with us, and find love with someone that shares our same love for Christ, rather than using His name or

His will to justify something that only we ourselves want. That is probably one of the most common methods by which we, as Western Christians, take His name in vain."

Chapter 4 – Infatuation

So why missionary date? Is it because of a deep concern for the soul of the lost person? Is it because this person is your soul mate and God simply doesn't have a clue? Well, no.

The mere act of missionary dating compromises the witness to begin with. If the Christian is willing to give up their standards in dating, what else are they willing to give up?

As shown in the last chapter, missionary dating starts because of dissatisfaction with waiting for God's provision. Infatuation plays a major role in this as well.

In this chapter we will discuss infatuation. I will go over puppy love as well as the psychological definition of infatuation. I will also interview my pastor and his wife.

Interview: The Cepelas

Pastor Mike and Ana Cepela have been married for 25 years (as of 2009) and have four children. Pastor Mike is also the pastor of my church, New Life Assembly Church.

After service on Sunday morning, I managed to get an

interview with him and his wife. After eating lunch, I turned on my tape recorder and started with my questions.

Ana is originally from Mexico, but her family eventually moved to Texas. Her father was a Christian musician that toured various churches. When he decided to visit a church up north, Ana was in trade school. Her parents at first allowed her to stay for school. However, Ana's father decided to bring her at the last minute.

Mike decided to come out to his church for a worship concert. He was not planning on going out to church that night. In fact, it was the last night of the concert. As he was headed to church, he noticed a man stalled on the side of the road. He pulled over to help the man, which was out of character for him. The man turned out to be a Christian in Bible college, just like Mike. Mike brought him some jumper cables, and he was going to hang out with the young man. However, the man told Mike that he thought it was important that Mike continued to church that night.

That night, Mike met Ana. If neither of them came out that night, there was no chance of them meeting again. Something about Ana caught Mike's eye, although Mike didn't understand why at the time. God didn't tell him that night she was his wife, but there was a sense of something. At that time, Mike dated many within the Church, but there was no desire to rush things with Ana.

Ana knew from the Lord that she wouldn't marry within her ethnicity. And the night she met Mike she didn't know what to expect. She wasn't seeking for a relationship. She was simply hungry for God. Ana remembered how three months before she met Mike, she told the Lord that nothing else mattered but Him.

After service and worship, Mike walked in. There was a lot of commotion when he walked in, and Ana turned around and saw Mike. The Spirit of the Lord then said that was her mate. She replied with, "I wasn't looking for a mate!" Eventually, the Lord worked the relationship out, despite the fact Ana lived in Texas. Pastor Mike and Ana said they learned much through marriage, including patience, sacrifice and dependence on God.

Ana said that the spouse must be willing to hear the truth and be changed by the truth. She sees many couples that *say* they are honest with each other; however, they actually try not to rile each other up. In other words, they ignore each other's flaws and issues, instead of working to solve them.

"That is their way of dealing with the issues," Ana said. "But really, issues aren't being dealt with. It is like throwing a cover over the problem. It is like they are walking around the problem, making sure they don't step on it."

Pastor Mike believes that many Christian males would say their biggest challenge in marriage is good sex (if they answered honestly). However, Pastor Mike answered for himself saying that the biggest challenge in marriage is not asking your wife to fulfill something that only God can fulfill. Another challenge he noted was disregarding the world's view of marriage.

"The model of the world has two people living under one roof," Pastor Mike said. "The model for the Body is one flesh."

Pastor Mike said that moving as one unit in marriage isn't difficult, but we make it difficult. Many couples think that because they are Christians, they will automatically move in synch. Pastor Mike notes that in his 25 years of marriage, he is hard pressed to say he always moved in harmony with his wife.

Ana advises young people to go back to their foundation in Christ before getting into a serious relationship. She said that if you don't understand the plan God has for you, you might lose yourself in the other person when you do get married. She continued to say that your identity in Christ and call for your life all affect your relationships. Singles should listen to their parents, Ana notes. She stated to not listen to peers, as most are not married. Peers will lead you wrong, Ana says, as they themselves are immature.

Pastor Mike said that it is not wrong for a single Christian to want to get married. However, Jesus needs to be enough.

"If I'm in Christ, but I am totally depressed all the time because I don't have a mate, that shouldn't be," Pastor Mike said. "What I advise to that person is definitely don't marry in that stage, because you are going to ask your mate to bring you an emotional state that she's not even capable of, because you don't even know how to enjoy the love of God. Part of how I enjoy God, I can share [that] with my mate. But, if I lack that, think about the burden I place on her."

I asked Ana if there was anything wrong with a single person complaining about their singlehood. She replied that she doesn't think that there is anything wrong with that. It might just be simple curiosity. However, the problem comes in when a person acts upon the desire.

"God's working on your character in everything," Ana said. "It's not so much that you are bad, or you are not ready. I think it is just God working His character in you in all aspects of your personality. To me, I think it is a blessing."

The Cepelas even clarified that waiting process could be God's dealing with the Christian, in that it strains the Christian to trust and rely fully on God.

Pastor Mike and Ana have seen infatuation taint many relationships down throughout the years. Pastor Mike notes how infatuation tends to be highly physical. It tends to lead to fornication, quick divorces and even violence.

"It always weakens the couples effectiveness of even their own Christian walk," Pastor Mike said. "It always distracts them. Couples should come together with a God given mate in a God given union, producing glory for the Kingdom of God. But what we seen with infatuation is an intensity to where the person becomes the full object of attention, adoration and everything."

Pastor Mike related the bitterness that follows infatuation to the hatred Amnon had for Tamar. 2 Samuel 13:15 says that the hatred with which Amnon hated Tamar was greater than the love with which he loved her.

"When somebody is infatuated, you got to think about what they are infatuated with," Ana said. "A lot of the time, it is not the person they think they are in love with, but it's the role and what that role portrays. It's not the heart of the person, or God's heart in that person."

Ana described infatuation as a mirage of a marriage and a relationship. In other words, it creates an illusion of what a person is actually like. She visited a conference for pastor's wives several years back. It was a sad time, though it did open her eyes as well as confirm some of her observations. Ana kept on hearing how wives married into the relationship not knowing what to expect. In other words, they married a role. They did not marry the person. There was no mention of God speaking. Some of the wives married the husbands because they grew up in the same church.

"And then you are hearing all their problems that they want counsel and wisdom in," Ana said. "And it's like, no wonder the marriages are a mess: because God didn't direct it, God didn't plan it, and God obviously didn't bring this thing together."

"We've seen nothing but empty godlessness coming out of infatuative relationships," Pastor Mike continued. "Violating moral boundaries, losing sight of good friends, losing sight of godly counsel and wisdom."

Puppy Love

Infatuation is a state of passion based on fantasy; it is intense and normally short-lived. Synonyms include "being in love" or having a "crush".

I'm sure most readers have been infatuated at one time or another. This is probably most evident during childhood, when it is called "puppy love". Boy meets girl. Girl meets boy. The boy's heart breaks for the girl. Boy gives a gift to the girl. Girl likes the gift. They fall in love, for about three days.

Years ago, I went to a church youth rally. There was a huge influx of younger boys in the youth group that year. After the games and preaching ended, the youth group stopped for ice cream.

One of the boys (who I believe was thirteen) said he had a girlfriend. He then asked me if I had one. I replied no. In my mind, it didn't seem right to take on a relationship without being ready for the responsibility.

The boy wondered in amazement at how someone older than him didn't have a girlfriend. He went on to tell me his girlfriend's name. I asked if he knew her last name. The boy didn't know; it apparently was too long. His father was with us and immediately jumped in. The father went on to describe how the girl's name was too long to fit on the caller ID. I was dumbfounded by the ridiculousness of it all.

Then, puppy love struck again! I came to a Sunday night service at a church early once. Some of the church women were talking and one of the younger girls appeared. At eleven years old, this girl said she had a boyfriend. She went on saying that she shouldn't get involved with anyone else. Years later on Facebook, I would find the girl's status fluctuating between *single* and *in a relationship*.

I'm not trying to be a party pooper. I don't believe anything sexual was going on in the examples mentioned. Although, I might be wrong, since sexual encounters are occurring at younger ages these days. But the mindset in these youth frightens me. Why can't they just be kids?

By youth, I mean any age group between being a child and high school graduation. Even after high school, a person still might not be mature enough to handle a serious relationship.

It isn't so much that these kids are dating. However, the parents approve (and in some cases, pressure) the kids to get into serious relationships young. Note that these parents are Christian; some are even leaders in the Church.

Why would the parents pressure these children at such a young age? I must note again that my concern is not for the world. The presence of relationships based on puppy love is within the people of God as well.

When we allow children to get involved in a serious relationship before maturity, something dire happens. The children get trained to find the "perfect one" through multiple relationships. They become insensitive and mocking of waiting on God and His provision.

Youth can be spent doing better things. 1 Timothy 4:12 says *let no one despise your youth, but be an example to the believers in word, in conduct, in love, in spirit, in faith, in purity.*

Teenagers are in a particularly special time of their life. While they don't have all the responsibilities of an adult, they can do certain things like an adult. This is a crucial time in a Christian's walk. There are many things that the youth can do, that they can't do later in life. Some older Christians I know (even some interviewed for this book) regret not doing more things for God in their youth. The adult life of marriage, work and their own kids restricts one's ability to do certain things.

Some parents (as stated before) do not help the situation either. My grandmother is something else when it comes to my love life. Every so often she would ask my mother if I have a girlfriend. One day, while shopping in a grocery store, my grandmother asked my Mom when I was going to have a girlfriend, so that I may get her some great-grandchildren.

My Mom explained that I wanted to get out of college first. However, my grandmother refused to hear it. Instead, she insisted that many other young people are having relationships and children at my age. One person in line even turned around and agreed with my grandmother.

This may sound funny, but it is true. Some Christian parents carry a strange insecurity for their children to get into a relationship. This is not helped by the fact their peers are promiscuous.

Tennov and Limerence

In 1977, Dorothy Tennov, former professor of psychology at University of Bridgeport, Connecticut invented the term *Limerence*. Her book *Love and Limerence: The Experience of Being in Love* first used the word in 1979. Tennov describes limerence in one of the clearest ways possible.

Limerence is a form of infatuation. Tennov says that it begins usually at a point in time that is barely discernable, but able to be recalled. Once Limerence begins, the limerent person thinks about love interest with great delight.

Crystallization is another trait of Limerence. This occurs when the love interest's positive characteristics are magnified, and unattractive traits are ignored. In some cases, bad characteristics may even be seen as good. Everything that the love interest does is seen as good (at least to a point). The limerent person may miss very important traits or problems in the love interest. In missionary dating, this problem might be the person being lost.

Memories of interactions with the love interest are imprinted in the limerent person's memories. The limerent person is super-sensitive; in other words, there is a sustained alertness and heightened awareness on the actions of the love interest.

Fear makes the limerent person move with caution, not wanting to feel full rejection. When reciprocation is perceived, extreme happiness is felt. Thoughts are focused on considering and reconsidering the attractive traits of the limerent other. Also, the limerent person replays interactions with the love interest in their mind.

If the limerent person doubts the love interest's reciprocation or if external obstacles increase, interaction with the love interest is increased. It can even reach a point where interaction is not impossible.

Eventually, fantasies are preferred to reality, unless the limerent person is acting in a way to win the love interest's heart or being in the presence of the love interest. This "relationship" continues when there is both a reason to hope and doubt the love interest's reciprocation.

If reciprocation is perceived, involvement decreases. The best way to cure reciprocation, as Tennov says, is prevention. Once emotions take control, you are at the mercy of external situations. The only true action against limerence is destruction of any opportunity for reciprocation to occur (Tennov).

Note again, that this is a secular psychologist's view on infatuation. As Christians, we are not bound to follow in the footsteps of the world. However, we still can get caught up, if we permit ourselves to.

Is Infatuation Love?

Limerence is a form of infatuation. As mentioned, crystallization and uncertainty of reciprocation play major roles in limerent thinking. So is infatuation love? Based on the previous definitions, it is obvious that love and infatuation don't really blend too well together.

Despite what the movies and the world tell us, extreme infatuation and love are not the same. Even by their characteristics, one can see that infatuation is very self motivated.

Michelle Drew of *PsychCentral* included lack of trust and lack of commitment as common traits of infatuation. Other traits include impatience, doubt, envy and an overall instability.

Let us compare these traits of infatuation to a few verses in the

Scripture. Some of these verses relate to true love.

Infatuation doesn't trust. In fact, it is distrustful of the very object it desires attention from. Infatuation does not trust the Lord for love. Instead, it takes matters into its own hands.

Psalms 37:5 says, *commit your way to the Lord, trust also in Him, and He shall bring [it] to pass.* In contrast, the infatuated person places their trust in the flesh (Jeremiah 17:5). This is done in two ways: infatuated people trust in themselves and in the object of affection for reciprocation.

Infatuation is impatient. It desires reciprocation as soon as possible, instead of being patient on the Lord. Psalms 37:7 says, *rest in the Lord, and wait patiently for Him; do not fret because of him who prospers in his way, because of the man who brings wicked schemes to pass.*

Having faith that the Lord will make provision for a mate tests our faith (James 1:4). Infatuation when it is out of control does not desire to be patient. We can even look back at Pastor Mike's testimony. Although he could spot something different about Ana, he didn't take matters into his own hands. He was able to wait.

Infatuation is heavily based on fantasy. Moreover, infatuation is based on what the infatuated person thinks is going to happen. It is also based on an imagined version of the object of affection.

This emphasis on fantasy reminds me of Luke 12:19. Jesus speaks of a certain rich man. The rich man said, *and I will say to my soul, "Soul, you have many goods laid up for many years; take your ease; eat, drink, [and] be merry."*

Later in the passage we find that the Lord required his soul of him that night. I don't think God is going to strike anyone dead for being infatuated. Nevertheless, the infatuated person makes assumptions that are unrealistic and uncertain.

Infatuation is unstable. The emotions of the infatuated person fluctuate highly between happiness and despair. And these are all based on the reciprocation of the object. Infatuation is by its very nature unstable.

Ephesians 3:17-19 says,

17. That Christ may dwell in your hearts through faith; that you, being rooted and grounded in love, 18. may be able to comprehend with all the saints what [is] the width and length and depth and height-- 19. to know the love of Christ which passes knowledge; that you may be filled with all the fullness of God.

Note how Paul writes that true love roots and grounds the believer. So, stability is a trait of love. This is especially true for the love of Christ. However, infatuation is like an emotional rollercoaster.

Infatuation idealizes the other person. Tennov explained that within crystallization, the infatuated person hyper-focuses on the positive traits of the object of affection. The infatuated person downplays or ignores the negative traits.

Romans 2:23 says, *for all have sinned and fall short of the glory of God.* Everyone is a sinner, even the object of the infatuated person's affection. The infatuated person maybe in for a great letdown when they discover that the person who they see as perfect is in fact very flawed (just like everyone else).

Finally, infatuation demands reciprocation. This is the most crucial point I need to make about infatuation. As stated with Limerence, when the infatuated person doubts the object of affection's love, it will intensify interaction with the object.

As a result, infatuation can be broken down into a desire for a response. Although it may start innocent, infatuation can grow exponentially. Extreme infatuation can consume a considerable amount of energy and time. A person can quite possibly be focused on whom they desire from dawn to dusk. And any desire that God says a person shouldn't have is sin. This will be discussed more in the next chapter.

Ending Infatuation

So, if you are caught in infatuation, are you a wicked sinner condemned to Hell? I don't think so.

In other words, if God sends your wife or your husband, chances are you will have moments of infatuation. However, they are *moments* of infatuation. To base a whole relationship on the initial feeling of being in love is dangerous. And to confuse infatuation with true love shows extreme immaturity.

So what do you do if you are caught in an infatuation and you want to get out? Believers have the advantage of prayer. If the believer becomes aware of the fact they are infatuated, they can ask the Lord to end their misdirected attention.

Chapter 5 – Lust

We see that infatuation is in fact more based on a desire for reciprocation, and thus is related more to lust than true love. Usually, the modern term *lust* is associated with sexual desire. In reality, lust can really be any desire that goes against the will or character of God

Most lust starts from a natural desire. For instance, a man's desire for a woman is natural. However, Satan takes that which is natural, and perverts it. Missionary dating, despite its best ambitions, falls into the category of lustful desires. This is due to the fact that the believer desires a relationship with someone that God forbids.

Sex isn't Bad

It should be noted that sex in itself is not bad. However, God designed sex to be enjoyed under certain conditions. Sex is meant to glorify God (1 Corinthians 6:20); it is only properly expressed in a marriage between a husband and a wife. 1 Corinthians 7:2 says, *because of sexual immorality, let each man have his own wife, and let each woman have her own husband.* Sex outside the confines of marriage between a man and a woman violates God's design.

There are four main purposes for sex. The first and most

obvious purpose is for procreation. Genesis 1:28 says, *then God blessed them, and God said to them, "Be fruitful and multiply; fill the earth and subdue it; have dominion over the fish of the sea, over the birds of the air, and over every living thing that moves on the earth."*

Second, sex is an expression of intimacy. Song of Solomon 2:6 says, *his left hand [is] under my head, and his right hand embraces me.*

Third, sex is an expression of companionship. Song of Solomon 3:1 says, *by night on my bed I sought the one I love; I sought him, but I did not find him.*

Fourth, sex is a means of physical pleasure. Song of Solomon 1:2 says, *let him kiss me with the kisses of his mouth-- for your love [is] better than wine.*

I write all of this to say that the Bible doesn't present sex as being bad. It is not to be ignored or seen as something ugly. Only the context in which sex is expressed makes it bad or good.

Some theologians think that the sexual union represents the intimacy of the Trinity. Christian Apologetics Research and Ministry (CARM) said, "This is not to say that the members of the Godhead, the Father, Son and Holy Spirit, have sexual relations. That is absurd. But there is an incredible intimacy and communion between them."

The three Persons of the Godhead are one. Jesus said in John 10:30 that He and the Father are one. Genesis 2:24 say that when a man and woman are married, they are to become one flesh.

"This expression of physical union which has a spiritual aspect to it (the two become one flesh) and is why some theologians see the sexual relation as a sacred experience," said CARM.

Sexuality is a gift from God. Sex and the marriage bed are to remain holy and undefiled (Hebrews 13:4). The sacredness of sexuality goes completely opposite of a society that uses sex as a means of advertising and entertainment. The marriage bed must not violate God's law in deed or thought. This means no adultery (Matthew 5:27-28), homosexuality (Romans 1:26-28), or sex before marriage (fornication, 1 Corinthians 6:9-10). Sex must be experienced according to God's design. Otherwise, it will not completely fulfill God's plan for pleasure and intimacy.

Lust Defined

As stated before, Satan takes the natural sexual desire, and perverts it. In reality, lust is any desire for something that God forbids. It can really be for anything, like money or attention.

James 1:14-16 says,

14. But each one is tempted when he is drawn away by his own desires and enticed. 15. Then, when desire has conceived, it gives birth to sin; and sin, when it is full-grown, brings forth death. 16. Do not be deceived, my beloved brethren.

Sin's end result is death. Lust entices people with false promises. It burns like a fire (Isaiah 57:5), and visual stimuli only acts like gasoline. Lust promises satisfaction outside the will of God; however, it leaves the lustful heart empty and unfulfilled.

Verse 16 continues into the rest of James. Therefore, it brings up a point about lust that I find interesting. Self-deception is interrelated with lust. There is a quote from an advertising documentary that always intrigued me. One of the researchers in the documentary studied how ads influenced the consumer. He said, "The key to all persuasion, is to make the person persuade themselves."

A person entangled in lust is not fully aware of the ramifications of what they are doing. This is due to the fact they are self-deceived. If the person knew what was truly happening (like, the end result of lust being death), they would not be deceived. Consequently, the Devil makes the person deceive him or herself. The Devil makes people believe they need something that will kill them.

There are two kinds of lust. These are the lust of the flesh, and lust of the eyes.

1 John 2:15-17 says,

15. Do not love the world or the things in the world. If anyone loves the world, the love of the Father is not in him. 16. For all that [is] in the world--the lust of the flesh, the lust of the eyes, and the pride of life--is not of the Father but is of the world. 17. And the world is passing away, and the lust of it; but he who does the will of God abides forever.

Lust of the flesh involves the physical urges of the body, and is more internal. This also includes faulty thought processes. Lust of the eyes involves the "looking" aspect or what we see. This is the external aspect of lust. Lust of the flesh and eyes are both temporal, due to their being in this temporal world. So where does this desire start?

Matthew 5:27-29 says,

27. "You have heard that it was said to those of old, 'You shall not commit adultery.' 28. But I say to you that whoever looks at a woman to lust for her has already committed adultery with her in his heart. 29. If your right eye causes you to sin, pluck it out and cast [it] from you; for it is more profitable for you that one of your members perish, than for your whole body to be cast into hell.

We see that ungodly desire starts in the heart. Jeremiah 17:9-10 says that the heart is deceitful and desperately wicked. Matthew 15:19 says that evil thoughts, adulteries and fornication precede out of the heart.

Jesus brings things deeper than just the glance at a woman. He brings it down to the heart. Are we supposed to physically pluck out our eyes then? Obviously not, but Jesus shows the gravity of what lust can do. Lust brings people to Hell.

A pastor once told me of a young man who said that once he got married, that would end all his sexual frustrations. The pastor said that it was only the beginning.

Why did the pastor correct this young man's thinking? It is because his true problem wasn't a need for a wife. His real problem was his lust hindering his relationship with Jesus. External factors, like marriage, will not help. If the only reason this young man was getting married was to stop his sexual frustrations, then things will get worse. Lust is a problem of the heart.

Pastor Mike Cepela even noted how the matter of the heart is related to believing and lust. Romans 10:10 says, *for with the heart one believes unto righteousness, and with the mouth confession is made unto salvation.* Pastor Mike noted that if believing in Christ results in righteousness, what does believing in lust bring about?

Lust is too often confused for love; however, love and lust are complete opposites. Love gives, whereas lust takes. Love is selfless, whereas lust is selfish.

Lust enslaves us to our desires. Romans 6:12 says, *therefore do not let sin reign in your mortal body, that you should obey it in its lusts.*

Porn addicts have confessed that once lust has started, it is difficult to stop. Sexual desires dictate the schedule. Porn addicted husbands would stay up late, and alone looking at images while their wives sleep alone. Time is wasted. All other concerns take a backdrop to the terrible flame of lust.

Lust causes hatred of self. Ezekiel 6:9 says, *and they that escape of you shall remember me among the nations whither they shall be captives, because I am broken with their whorish heart, which hath departed from me, and with their eyes, which go a whoring after their idols: and they shall loathe themselves for the evil which they have committed in all their abominations.*

Lust causes the believer and nonbeliever to hate himself. Similarly, common traits of those addicted to porn are low-self esteem, guilt, introversion, self-consciousness, fear and depression.

Why does lust cause self-hatred? First, this is because lust is based on self. Fulfilling lust only causes the attention to be brought back on self, not on anyone else. Second, the heart that lusts knows it deserves punishment. The heart that lusts (if not seared) still has a conscience (Hebrews 10:27).

A Soul Tie

Sex, whether under God's provision or not, unites.

A soul tie is a bond between a person and something else. That something can be another person, an idol, or even an evil spirit. Like the Trinity, the term *soul tie* is not in the Bible, though it is inferred.

David and Jonathan had a good soul tie based on friendship (1 Samuel 18:1). A godly marriage is an example of a good soul tie, where both individuals work towards following Jesus (Matthew 19:5). Good Christian fellowship also creates productive soul ties.

For example, Colossians 2:2 says, *that their hearts might be comforted, being knit together in love, and unto all riches of the full understanding, to the acknowledgment of the mystery of God, and of the Father, and of Christ.* Take note of the phrase *knit together*.

However, negative soul ties can occur as well. Sex outside of marriage can result in a soul tie. Unhealthy relationships characterized by emotional abuse, dependency, guilt, and manipulation can result in a soul tie. When a believer heavily invests into a harmful relationship, a soul tie can occur. Still, even if sex is absent, a dating relationship can grow into an "emotional" marriage.

Sexual abuse and molestation can cause a soul tie. Such a victim must seek restoration through prayer and trusted Christians, in order to prevent future underlying problems.

Pornography can create a soul tie. It may not occur in every instance, but the risk is always there. A person can be joined to an image or an evil spirit.

Hosea 4:17 reads, *Ephraim is joined to idols: let him alone.* Idols caused separation for Ephraim from healing.

"Note, it is a sad and sore judgment for any man to be let alone in sin, for God to say concerning a sinner, "He is joined to his idols, the world and the flesh; he is incurably proud, covetous, or profane, an incurable drunkard or adulterer; *let him alone;* conscience, let him alone; minister, let him alone; providences, let him alone," said Matthew Henry in one of his commentaries. "Let nothing awaken him till the flames of hell do it (Henry)."

Because lust might be involved with the soul tie, self-deception might be involved. Nevertheless, there are a few things that can be used to gauge if there is a soul tie.

First, take a moment and ask the Lord in prayer if you have any soul ties. If He shows you any, pray that the soul tie would be severed in the name of Jesus.

Second, look at the fruit. If a relationship is a bad soul tie, it will produce bad fruit (Matthew 7:16-18). A good soul tie will strengthen our walk with God. A bad soul tie will bear fruits of hatred, resentment, manipulation, anger and bitterness. Compare the works of the relationship with Galatians 5:19-21. The overall fruit of a bad soul tie will dampen (and even destroy) our walk with God.

A bad soul tie must be cut through prayer. The Christian must identify the sin source and repent. If it is an object, the object must be destroyed and removed from the home. After this, pray for the restoration of your spirit from any negative effects (Cook). Further means of prevention and recovery will be discussed in the upcoming chapters.

Chapter 6 – Samson and Solomon

I believe that no two people in the Bible show the downfalls of lust more than Samson and Solomon. Despite the one's supernatural strength and the other's great wisdom, both gave into their sensual desires. As a result, both paid dearly.

The Strength of Samson

Samson was the son of Manoah, an Israelite from the tribe of Dan. Samson was the twelfth Judge of Israel. The Judges were leaders during a period of strong disobedience, between the conquest of Canaan and the formation of the first Kingdom of Israel.

Judges 13 describes how Manoah and his wife had no children. An angel appeared to the barren wife, and stated that she will conceive a child who will be a deliverer of Israel (Judges 13:5). Note how God sent an angel to herald the birth of Samson. This doesn't even occur to other prominent people in the Bible. However, Samson was meant for something more.

Again, note how the writer uses the terms the *Angel of the Lord* (Judges 13:13) and *Man of God* (13:8). The *Angel of the Lord* sometimes refers to the pre-incarnate Jesus. So, is this the pre-incarnate Jesus here in Judges? It is debatable. However, if it is Jesus, how many people does the Lord Himself come herald the birth of, let alone an angel?

Samson was separated as a Nazirite. Nazirites took the vow of asceticism as described in Numbers 6:1-21. They abstained from alcohol, refrained from the cutting off of hair, and avoided corpses and graves.

Although Samson was separated as a Nazirite, he still kept carnal connections. Judges 14:1-3 describes his desire to choose a wife from the Philistines, instead of the Israelites. Of course, Samson is known for his downfall with Delilah.

Judges 16:1-4 says,

1. Now Samson went to Gaza and saw a harlot there, and went in to her. 2. When the Gazites were told, "Samson has come here!" they surrounded the place and lay in wait for him all night at the gate of the city. They were quiet all night, saying, "In the morning, when it is daylight, we will kill him." 3. And Samson lay low till midnight; then he arose at midnight, took hold of the doors of the gate of the city and the two gateposts, pulled them up, bar and all, put them on his shoulders, and carried them to the top of the hill that faces Hebron. 4. Afterward it happened that he loved a woman in the Valley of Sorek, whose name [was] Delilah.

Empowered by the Lord, Samson had tremendous strength. Verse 3 says that he pulled the gateposts and the gate of the city on his shoulders. Samson was spiritual at times. Judges 15:14 says that *the*

Spirit of the Lord came mightily upon him, in order to break the ropes of the Philistines.

However, Samson loved Delilah. Samson loved someone who was not spiritually aligned to the God of Israel. In addition, Samson let someone close to his heart that actually meant to harm him. Did he know that Delilah meant to harm him? Judges 16:6-14 makes it obvious that Samson did know, however, it didn't matter. His lust blinded him.

Judges 16:15-17 says,

15. Then she said to him, "How can you say, 'I love you,' when your heart [is] not with me? You have mocked me these three times, and have not told me where your great strength [lies]." 16. And it came to pass, when she pestered him daily with her words and pressed him, [so] that his soul was vexed to death, 17. that he told her all his heart, and said to her, "No razor has ever come upon my head, for I [have been] a Nazirite to God from my mother's womb. If I am shaven, then my strength will leave me, and I shall become weak, and be like any [other] man."

All of his God-given strength was meaningless in the sight of his lust. His lust revealed his weakness. He tolerated Delilah's pestering, and she took advantage of it. Likewise, the Devil will take any advantage we can offer him. I once heard a pastor say that if you give Satan an inch, he will take a mile.

Judges 16:19-21 says,

> *19. Then she lulled him to sleep on her knees, and called for a man and had him shave off the seven locks of his head. Then she began to torment him, and his strength left him. 20. And she said, "The Philistines [are] upon you, Samson!" So he awoke from his sleep, and said, "I will go out as before, at other times, and shake myself free!" But he did not know that the Lord had departed from him. 21. Then the Philistines took him and put out his eyes, and brought him down to Gaza. They bound him with bronze fetters, and he became a grinder in the prison.*

Delilah lulled Samson to sleep. He was insensitive to the fact that the Lord left him. The Philistines put out his eyes and took him to Gaza. Likewise, lust can cause us to be spiritually asleep. We can be completely unaware that the power of God has left us. But we may still continue as if nothing happened. Lust can cause us to be completely blind to the things of the Spirit.

The hair and the faith of Samson did begin to grow back (Judges 16:22). The mercy of God allowed him to accomplish one last miracle of strength. One can't help but wonder how much more Samson could have accomplished? He became an example of Proverbs 25:28, which says, *whoever [has] no rule over his own spirit [is like] a city broken down, without walls.* What more could this Judge heralded by an angel have done if not controlled by his desire?

Samson was gifted with strength; however, Solomon was gifted with wisdom.

The Wisdom of Solomon

Solomon was the son of David and Bathsheba. He was the third King of Israel and the writer of most of the book of Proverbs. Solomon is also credited as the writer of Ecclesiastes and the Song of Solomon. He was also the builder of the First Temple in Jerusalem (1 Kings 5-6).

Although he married Pharaoh's daughter due to treaty with Egypt, Solomon did love the Lord (1 Kings 3:1-3).

1 Kings 3:5-10 says,

5. At Gibeon the Lord appeared to Solomon in a dream by night; and God said, "Ask! What shall I give you?" 6. And Solomon said: "You have shown great mercy to Your servant David my father, because he walked before You in truth, in righteousness, and in uprightness of heart with You; You have continued this great kindness for him, and You have given him a son to sit on his throne, as [it is] this day. 7. Now, O Lord my God, You have made Your servant king instead of my father David, but I [am] a little child; I do not know [how] to go out or come in. 8. And Your servant [is] in the midst of Your people whom You have chosen, a great people, too numerous to be numbered or counted. 9. Therefore give to Your servant an understanding heart to judge Your people, that I may discern between good and evil. For who is able to judge this great people of Yours?" 10. The speech pleased the Lord, that Solomon had asked this thing.

The Lord found Solomon's choice to be wise. Solomon was

humble and asked for understanding and discernment. Solomon carried tremendous insight, as evidenced by the Judgment of Solomon in 1 Kings 3:16-28.

1 Kings 4:29-34 describes the depth of Solomon's heart and wisdom. His wisdom excelled all the wisdom of his contemporaries. He spoke three thousand proverbs and one thousand and five songs. Kings from all over the world came to hear his wisdom. The Lord said He would give Solomon riches and honor on top of wisdom (1 Kings 3:13).

However, Solomon made a fatal error similar to that of Samson. Where as Samson joined himself to a harlot, Solomon joined himself to many foreign wives.

1 Kings 11:1-4 says,

1. But King Solomon loved many foreign women, as well as the daughter of Pharaoh: women of the Moabites, Ammonites, Edomites, Sidonians, and Hittites-- 2. from the nations of whom the Lord had said to the children of Israel, "You shall not intermarry with them, nor they with you. Surely they will turn away your hearts after their gods." Solomon clung to these in love. 3. And he had seven hundred wives, princesses, and three hundred concubines; and his wives turned away his heart. 4. For it was so, when Solomon was old, that his wives turned his heart after other gods; and his heart was not loyal to the Lord his God, as was the heart of his father David.

The Lord warned Solomon not to intermarry with the foreign woman as stated in verse 2. Maybe Solomon thought he could turn all of their hearts to the Lord? One could wonder; at any rate, it is an obvious warning of how a corrupt relationship can turn a believer away from Jesus.

The New Testament now forbids polygamy (1 Timothy 3:2 and Titus 1:6). In the Old Testament, polygamy was permitted (2 Samuel 12:8); however, Solomon allowed this freedom to divide his heart.

The lust for his foreign wives lead to his lust for their gods (1 Kings 11:5). He did not fully love the Lord (1 Kings 11:6). As a result, the worship of Chemosh and Molech were sanctioned in Israel (1 Kings 11:6).

Eventually, after Solomon's death, the kingdom of Israel split in two. This shows how lust may not have a direct effect on the person's own generation. Sadly, a person's lust can affect those they love as well as the generation after them.

"Solomon was a guide-post, rather than an example," one commentator said. "He pointed the way to wisdom, but in the latter part of his life he did not walk in it; hence his son Rehoboam, followed his example, rather than his counsels, and became a foolish and evil ruler (Thompson)."

Solomon, who the Lord appeared to twice, had turned his heart away to lust and idolatry (1 Kings 11:9,10). In the next chapter, we will discuss how idolatry and lust are interrelated.

Chapter 7 – Porn

Every second, nearly $3,075 is spent on pornography. Every second, 28,258 Internet users are viewing pornography. Every second, 372 Internet users are typing adult search terms into search engines.

There are roughly 72 million visitors to pornography a month. 4.2 million pornographic websites exist on the Internet, which is about 12% of all websites. And 47% of Christians say that porn is a problem in their home (Ropelato).

With the innovation of the Internet, the sex industry became one of the most profitable businesses in the world. Like the drug industry, the sex industry of porn feeds off the addictions of people. It destroys the lives of many, blurring the mind to the things of God and setting the stage for future strongholds.

This section focuses on lust in the form of pornography. The effects and destruction stories of porn will be addressed, as well as tips for recovery. It should be noted that these items could really be applied to any form of lust.

Pornography is Idolatry

There is a connection between human sexuality and worship. In the past, idol worship wasn't just about a man kneeling before a stone figurine. There was a sensual element often overlooked.

I really took notice of the connection between sexuality and idolatry when I read 1 Corinthians 10:6-8, which read:

6. Now these things became our examples, to the intent that we should not lust after evil things as they also lusted. 7. And do not become idolaters as [were] some of them. As it is written, "The people sat down to eat and drink, and rose up to play." 8. Nor let us commit sexual immorality, as some of them did, and in one day twenty-three thousand fell.

Paul wrote about the children of Israel, as evidenced by earlier verses in the chapter. Notice how Paul, after mentioning lust in verse 6, warns about idolatry in verse 7. Verse 8 warns against sexual immorality. Although, there is a distinction between sexual immorality and idolatry, there also appears to be a connection. Let's continue to read verses 12 through 14.

12. Therefore let him who thinks he stands take heed lest he fall. 13. No temptation has overtaken you except such as is common to man; but God [is] faithful, who will not allow you to be tempted beyond what you are able, but with the temptation will also make the way of escape, that you may be able to bear [it]. 14. Therefore, my beloved, flee from idolatry.

Verse 12 starts with an address to pride. Anyone can fall, especially those who think they are okay. Verse 13 goes into how temptation can be withstood. But, verse 14 quickly and concisely says to flee idolatry.

Catch the connection there? The word *therefore* means that as a result of temptation by idols, the reader must (therefore) flee idols. You can see then a connection between temptation and idolatry. When I first read this, I wondered, "Why would an ancient reader be tempted to worship idols? Is there an aspect of desire that I am missing here?"

The reader must take into account how sexuality is historically related to idol worship. During the time of Paul, Corinth was known for its licentious nature (Thompson). The Temple of Aphrodite was said to serve 1000 temple prostitutes in Corinth (Strabo). So, the temptation to worship idols makes sense. This is because idolatry did not just constitute chanting to a stone figure; sexuality played a role as well.

Obviously, idolatry is condemned, as written in the Ten Commandments.

Exodus 20:3-6 says,

3. You shall have no other gods before Me. 4. You shall not make for yourself a carved image--any likeness [of anything] that [is] in heaven above, or that [is] in the earth beneath, or that [is] in the water under the earth: 5. you shall not bow down to them nor serve them. For I, the Lord your God, [am] a jealous God, visiting the iniquity of the fathers upon the children to the third and fourth [generations] of those who hate Me, 6. but showing mercy to thousands, to those who love Me and keep My commandments.

Idolatry is worshipping anything besides the true God. We can do this blatantly by worshipping false gods, such as a stone statue. Or we can do this subtly, by worshipping money or our own thinking.

The worship of sex, another person and an image all fall into idolatry. And all three of these constitute the essence of pornography.

Interview: Porn Free

Years ago, a grade school boy named Paul Cook saw pornography for the very first time. His friends brought adult magazines over. In college, he sought out porn even more.

"I was consumed with the desire for sex and allowed lust to control my mind," Paul remembered. "Since I did well academically and had an attractive girlfriend, my pride became an additional foothold for the Devil."

Paul continued to chase after women, until he finally got married. He thought that finally his lust and porn addiction would be broken. Paul sadly found out that he was wrong.

"I remember my heart racing with adrenaline as I purchased

porn mags from the local convenience store, slightly fearful that I might see someone from church." said Paul.

By this time, Paul was a youth leader and involved with ministry; however, this (or the fear of being caught) did not stop him. After enjoying the porn for a few days, he would throw it away in shame, promising to never look at it again. Eventually after a few weeks, he desired more. The lustful images never completely satisfied his heart.

The Internet opened a whole new world of temptation to Paul. He could visit porn sites anytime he wished, in private and for free. He planned to surf the web either when his wife left or when she went to bed. His addiction slowly consumed everything.

Paul felt the Holy Spirit convicting his heart. He realized he was leading a double life: a righteous Christian on the outside, and a porn addict on the inside.

"I knew it was wrong to look at porn and fantasize about sex," Paul said. "But it seemed difficult to stop. I could go for 2 or 3 months of sobriety before falling again. It seemed like an endless cycle."

Paul realized that he built up a sexual stronghold. He built the stronghold up with years of porn, sexual imaginations, and masturbation. His memories provided a constant source of temptation. His addictions weaken his marriage and damaged his sex life. He desired to see the lifeless images more than his own wife.

"One night in July 1998 at around 2 AM, I could not sleep," Paul said. "I felt a strong prompting to ask God for help in getting free of my sex addiction."

Instead of going onto the computer to surf for porn, Paul went to the living room and got on his knees to pray. He confessed his sin and desire to be free to Jesus. He asked for forgiveness and help. After this genuine prayer, Paul was able to fall asleep. The next morning, something changed.

"God had done a wonderful work in me," Paul said. "I was different. Somehow God changed me such that I could resist the urges to view porn and masturbate. I have been completely free of sex addiction since that night!"

The years since that night, this man learned how much the Holy Spirit plays a role in helping and healing the Christian. God taught Paul how to believe in sexual purity.

Soon after his freedom from sexual addiction, God inspired him to start a website. The site name is *Porn Free* (www.porn-free.org), a play on popular keywords that draw thousands through search engines.

I managed to get an interview with Paul Cook. During this interview, I asked him why he created the site, as well as advice for those dealing with sexual bondage.

Paul created the site in order to share what God did in his life concerning sexual addiction. He also wanted to share what he was learning about living for God, especially in the years after his initial freedom.

In the article *How Porn Works*, Paul notes how there are two forms of lust people are tempted by. 1 John 2:15-17 mentioned "lust of the eyes" and "lust of the flesh". Pornography encourages both by providing visual stimulation, that appeals to our fleshly desire for sex. It also offers lifelong fuel for lust through the memories of sexual images.

"With the help of special hormones released in the brain during sexual arousal, porn images are retained in our memories much longer than non-sexual memories." said Paul.

Destruction

Pornography can have a devastating effect on a person, whether Christian or lost. Pornography leaves the viewer craving more and more in order to achieve the same "sexual high".

"It easily enslaves people to their own cravings and opens the door to other forms of evil, like anger, abuse, violence, hatred, lying, envy, compulsiveness and selfishness," said Paul. "The power behind porn is revealed when the porn addict tries to stop their habit – it is virtually impossible without help."

Pornography is a world of fantasy. There are many lies that help sustain the fantasy. This fantasy is supported through imagery, depictions and scenarios. These work together to form a false world in the porn addict's mind that affects how he or she relates to real people.

"In short, the addict's world becomes increasingly sexualized, as sexualized material becomes the primary input of his or her mind," Paul said. "As the addict moves deeper into the porn fantasy world, they grow increasingly distant from 'normal' relationships and look for ways to act out that which they have been viewing in the fantasy world."

Sex addition can lead to strange behaviors. The extremes include promiscuity, pedophilia, anonymous sex, fetishes, bisexuality, sadomasochism, abductions, rape and even murder.

"These themes are popularized in pornography," said Paul. "Addicts who fantasize about such themes will eventually want to act them out in real life."

Pornography encourages the drive to serve one's self. As a result, it can affect the ability to give and receive true love. It can damage relationships, and increase the chance of a spouse or child finding the material. This in turn can cause a generational sin. Porn may invoke sexual frustration, lying, abuse, and irrational thinking in the viewer. A reader may want to take time to view the destruction stories on the *Porn-Free* site.

"Looking at pornography can damage the viewer's current or future marriage sex life," said *Porn-Free*. "Porn viewers may find that it's difficult to enjoy true intimacy with their spouse when they're fantasizing about somebody else! Additionally, porn builds an unrealistic perception of sexual relations. Porn sex is a portrayal or an act made for the viewer's enjoyment. It takes what God intended as a private expression of love between a husband and wife and prostitutes it for entertainment."

Porn-Free noted other side effects of pornography. These include irritability, uncontrolled thoughts, spiritual oppression, fear, guilt, condemnation, hopelessness, depression, and spiritual death.

Road to Recovery

Pornography is based on lies and the Devil is the father of lies (John 8:44). Lies make temptation appear more acceptable. The lies of the Devil must be met with the truth of the Word. John 8:31-32 says, *if you abide in My word, you are My disciples indeed. And you shall know the truth, and the truth shall make you free.* Spending time in His word is crucial for victory.

Porn-Free answered several lies with Scripture on the *Lies about sex sin, addiction and freedom* Page. Three lies/answers have been duplicated here:

Lie: "I'll never get free of sex addiction." Truth: Jesus died on the cross so we CAN get free of whatever sin struggle we are involved in. The Holy Spirit, who raised Christ from the dead, gives life to our mortal body so we can live in freedom (Romans 8:11,13). Life through Jesus Christ brings spiritual renewal and a new nature that enables us to walk in purity, just as Jesus did (2 Corinthians 5:17). No matter how bad we may have sinned, we can still come to Jesus and receive forgiveness and cleansing. Jesus' blood covers all our sins. Hebrews 6:17-20 affirms that we have hope in Jesus, who is the anchor of our soul.

Lie: "God won't accept me because I keep falling to temptation." Truth: Satan specializes in condemnation and despair. Once he entices us to sin, he condemns us for sinning, telling us we'll never be free. He tells us we'll never be able to please God. Jesus died so that we have peace with God. God is not angry with us for sinning, and he longs for us to accept Jesus' sacrifice and live in the reality of the new life he prepared for us. Jesus bore all of God's wrath due to us for our sin (Isaiah 53:4-12; Isaiah 54:10). God will not reject us when we approach him for help.

Lie: "Getting married will stop my pornography addiction." Truth: Marriage can make porn addiction worse, and porn addiction ruins a marriage's sex life! There are several reasons for this, but one of the key reasons is that porn addicts have sexually tuned themselves to respond to lust by porn pictures and masturbation. Married sex, by design, is to be built on love. Lust and love are total opposites! The porn addict should break his addiction before getting married.

Avoid sexually explicit movies and looking at people in a sexual manner. Pre-plan alternate activities to do when you feel the urge to view porn, such as calling a friend, exercise, prayer, worship or Bible reading. Remove things in your house that are related to porn.

"The hope of change and transformation comes through the power that Jesus brings to us when we place our faith in Him," Paul said. "The Scriptures say that if any person is in Christ, they become a new creation and receive the power of the Holy Spirit to live as a new person, no longer enslaved to former lusts and passion of the old creation (2 Corinthians 5:17)."

Christians can still default to old lusts. Transformation depends on the believer doing their part daily.

"Denying our flesh is something perhaps foreign to many people who live in societies such as the United States, where self-gratification is the soup du jour," Paul said. "Self-control is an alien concept and often not modeled or practiced by parents and leaders."

The Holy Spirit helps the believer in the area of self-control. Paul Cook described the Christian's relationship with the Holy Spirit as a kind of partnership. He does His part, provided we do our part. For example, the Holy Spirit will convict the Christian of sin. However, if the Christian ignores conviction, the conscience can grow calloused.

The Holy Spirit will convict us of areas in our lives where we need to grow in self-control. The Bible even mentions that one of the fruits of the Holy Spirit is self-control (Galatians 5:22-23).

"I believe this fruit grows as we exercise it – just like bodily exercise which strengthens our physical body, so will exercising self-control strengthen our ability to control our thoughts and urges," Paul said.

Thoughts and actions are key targets of self-control. If we can succeed in controlling the thoughts, controlling the actions will be much easier, as normally a thought leads an action. Thinking about committing a sin is tantamount to committing the sin. The Scripture exhorts us to take every thought captive to the obedience of Christ and to cast down every imagination that exalts itself against the knowledge of God (2 Corinthians 10:5).

"These are mental self-control exercises that we have the opportunity to perform daily," Paul said. "Practice makes perfect!"

Lastly, the law of sowing and reaping is particularly significant to the fight against sexual addictions and living the new life in Christ. If we sow to the desires of the flesh, we will reap some type of death in our lives. For example, it could be the death of innocence, the death of peace, or the death of a pure thought life. If we sow to the desires of the Holy Spirit, we will reap life and peace.

"This law underscores the need for us to break the habits of the 'old man' and to put on the 'new man' daily," Paul said. "If we do not, we will continue to reap a harvest of death and destruction in life."

I urge spending time in prayer, asking the Lord to change you by the blood of Jesus. Ask the Lord to break the chains of the flesh and lust, in the name of Jesus. Ask the Lord to help you to walk in purity, and He will answer.

A Call to Flee

The final tip on fighting lust can be found in 2 Timothy 2:22. The verse says, *flee also youthful lusts; but pursue righteousness, faith, love, and peace with those who call on the Lord out of a pure heart.*

So, don't try and put up a fight against lust. Run! Paul says that God is faithful to provide a means of escape (1 Corinthians 10:13). If it is a form of media or even another person causing you to lust, cut it out of your life.

Note that the Bible doesn't just tell you to run anywhere. The Bible tells us to run to righteousness, faith, love and peace. Ironically, when we stay in lust we instead have unrighteousness, disbelief, and a lack of peace. Note the *"with them that call on the Lord from a pure heart"* references the need for the prayers of others in your fellowship.

Because singles have no outlet for their sexual urges, pornography and lust are major threats to their Christian walk. In the next chapter, we will discuss singlehood and how it can be used to glorify God.

Chapter 8 – Singlehood

One day, at a church meeting (not my present congregation), it was time for testimonies. During testimony time, people stand up in the sanctuary, and testify of what God has done for them.

One of the girls stood up and thanked God for her "Christian" boyfriend. Soon after that night, the boyfriend left her and church.

I thought I would try something a bit different. I stood up in the congregation, and praised God for giving me the strength to remain single for the present time. I sat down, and the pastor thanked me, and said something along the lines of God not calling everyone to be married.

"Wait," I thought as I sat in the congregation. "I didn't say I wanted to be celibate!"

Of course, I meant a temporary singlehood. I eventually want to be married. But for now, I must be content with being single.

In this chapter, we will address how the Church sees singles, along with an interview with one of my single friends. We will look at the lives of singles in the Bible and look at various aids for Christian singles. Finally, we will go over the most extensive passage about singlehood, 1 Corinthians 7:25-40.

Interview: Matt

Matt is 32 years old (as of the writing of the book). He is also single. He always searched for the truth. Matt felt like there was a counterfeit feel to the world. A committed atheist before his salvation, he felt as if everything was a joke.

Matt was raised in a Catholic family, along with his brother and sister. Growing up, there was a constant stress from his parents for Matt and his brother to have a girlfriend.

"Even as an unbeliever I thought, I am not going to put any pressure on my kid," Matt said. "If they are going to find a girl, they are going to find a girl. There was this ridiculous pressure of, Where's the girl, Where's the girl? It was hard."

Years later, God brought some Christians into Matt's life. He worked with them, and started seeing truth in them. Six months before he got saved, he started watching Christian films, particularly *Flywheel*. He says there was something about those movies that interested him. One night, as Matt contemplated the delusions of the world, he cried out to Jesus. Matt called up Pastor Jay Peters, and told the Pastor that he needed to get right with God.

I interviewed Matt because I wanted to hear the thoughts and frustrations of the average Christian single.

Matt notes that besides a few dates, he's always been single, even before he was saved. He said the few girls he dated seemed like robots programmed by the world.

"I have had many opportunities to get into a lot of relationships with a lot of women. A lot of them were too ditsy and there wasn't much there. I have watched men take advantage of women, but I couldn't do it."

Up until he got saved, Matt believed he was going to die a pathetic 32-year old virgin, but that he was going to die with honor.

Once Matt was saved, he found the battle between flesh and spirit to be daunting. However, he knew that true love wasn't getting into a marriage to satiate a physical desire.

"What's frightening is you can put yourself in the mindset of I need to married because of this [physical desire]," Matt said. "Because this is sinful and the only way this is legit is through marriage."

Matt believes that the purpose of marriage is to conform us to the image of Christ. In that light, he also said that romance without God are really two people using each other for their own self-desires. He believes that many younger people are simply "shacking up" due to the failed relationships of the previous generation.

"The irony is that when I talk to people online about fornication and saying you shouldn't do that, to them, it's so ordinary. It's so run-of-the-mill these days. It's so pathetic in the eyes of the world these days that I haven't fornicated yet. When I hear that the supposed first time of fornication is 12 to 14 year old, that is shocking to me. But, to the world it is no big deal."

Matt said that he is learning a lot from Pastor Jay Peters (who is mentioned throughout this book). He noted that a real husband calls the shots, but listens and cares for his wife. A real father also cares and prays with his children. Also, the husband must protect his family and stand up for his wife.

"I think the real reason why so many people in our church are not married is because they are not ready for marriage," Matt said. "They are putting God second. And God, out of His love, is not going to allow an idol to be thrown in front of you. God's way is the right way, even if we fight it."

Matt notes that it does get exhausting waiting for a wife at times. He said that it would be nice to have a partner. However, Matt doesn't believe he has met that person yet. Also, his finances make marriage seem miles away.

"I guess the perfect one is out there," Matt said. "The mindset I got to get over is that this is not about fulfilling a sexual desire, but having a true love relationship with a woman. I know there is a balance there, I pray to God many times to show me what true love for a woman is. I think it will be alright when she comes."

Matt said he doesn't expect Ms. Perfect. He hopes that when she comes, he will know it is her.

Matt hopes that God is going to bring someone into his life that is both physically and spiritually attractive. He said she must be a straight-up Christian. After surveying Christian dating sites, Matt found many profiles to be spiritually apathetic. No one seemed to be on fire for God.

"I've noticed over time, women who come into our church who look like prospects (in terms of marriage and age)," Matt said. "However, the Spirit was saying no. It was the first time when seeing a compromised Christian didn't appeal."

One of the things that confused Matt was the boundaries between how far is too far in terms of physical intimacy. Although he knows that sex before marriage is wrong, he wasn't sure about making out.

"I mean, where does it stop?" Matt said. "I think it would be too cold if I were friends with a woman that I was evangelizing with, and suddenly I'm like, well, you want to get married. You don't want to be a robot, but you also don't want to upset God."

Matt noted that he may be over-analyzing things, and that he didn't want to be legalistic. Matt said that at the end of the day, his first love is Christ and that he needs to seek His face before getting married. At the end of the interview, he said that he hopes to get married before the age of 40.

When I try to explain why I am waiting for a spouse to a lost friend, they often look at me with confusion. Why? Because they are of the world; this is expected. Sometimes, the world will mock and harass Christian ideas based on purity.

Unfortunately, the world's perception of singlehood has infected the people of God. Rebecca Grace states in an article about singleness, that when the church doesn't do singleness, singles don't do church.

"As a result, Christian singles are left to face a world without spiritual guidance from the body of Christ," Grace wrote. "Eventually, many compromise their beliefs, specifically in regards to sexual purity before marriage (Grace)."

As mentioned in the chapter about infatuation, some churches encourage their teens (and even pre-teens) to date as soon as possible. From my experience, there are some churches where, if you don't marry soon after high school (especially for a male), your sexual orientation may indirectly come under question. Obviously, this hyper-masculinity doesn't help matters much.

Are Singles Losers?

It's official. The Church thinks singles are losers.

The world has influenced us, even in super-conservative denominations. Even the outer appearance of religion doesn't protect from this bias.

We have come a long way from when the early Christians upheld celibacy. The Church at times even looks down on temporal singlehood, as I am in. Athanasius, the church father known for helping to establish the deity of Christ, was single for his entire life. During one of his returns from exile, Athanasius visited Alexandria, Egypt in 346 AD. Athanasius commented on young maidens and men devoting themselves to celibacy (Athanasius). Today, it seems like the only people who are devoting themselves to celibacy are Catholic priests.

We can even go through the Bible and see godly people who were devoted to celibacy or were single. We can start with the prophetess Ana.

Luke 2:36-38 says,

36. Now there was one, Ana, a prophetess, the daughter of Phanuel, of the tribe of Asher. She was of a great age, and had lived with a husband seven years from her virginity; 37. and this woman [was] a widow of about eighty-four years, who did not depart from the temple, but served [God] with fastings and prayers night and day.38. And coming in that instant she gave thanks to the Lord, and spoke of Him to all those who looked for redemption in Jerusalem.

Ana saw the Child Jesus when Mary and Joseph brought Him to Jerusalem to be presented to the Lord. As you can read, her devotion to God did not end when her husband passed away. Jeremiah, the Weeping Prophet, was called to a life of celibacy.

Jeremiah 16:1-4 says,

1. The word of the Lord also came to me, saying, 2. "You shall not take a wife, nor shall you have sons or daughters in this place." 3. For thus says the Lord concerning the sons and daughters who are born in this place, and concerning their mothers who bore them and their fathers who begot them in this land: 4. "They shall die gruesome deaths; they shall not be lamented nor shall they be buried, but they shall be like refuse on the face of the earth. They shall be consumed by the sword and by famine, and their corpses shall be meat for the birds of heaven and for the beasts of the earth."

In reading verse 3 and 4, one can say that God's call to Jeremiah to remain celibate was protection, as the children of the generation would be overtaken by famines and sword. However, the reader must also consider Jeremiah's ministry. Jeremiah was called to preach to a people who would not listen.

The Bible never says whether or not Paul the Apostle was married. Nevertheless, Paul states he had the gift of celibacy in 1 Corinthians 7:17. Thus one can assume that he wasn't married as of the writing of his letters. Some Christians think his wife might have passed away.

1 Corinthians 9:5 says, *have we not power to lead about a sister, a wife, as well as other apostles, and [as] the brethren of the Lord, and Cephas?* Paul says that he (and Barnabas) have the ability to take a wife. A godly wife would be helpful. But Paul sees the advantage of remaining single, as he would able to accomplish more without caring for the

events in the world, as discussed in 1 Corinthians 7:25-40.

The reader must not forget about the prophets who were imbued with the spirit of Elijah: Elijah himself, Elisha, and John the Baptist. I mention them because they lived a life of asceticism (Matthew 3:4). Asceticism is commonly associated with celibacy.

We may also mention Jesus Christ. During His earthly ministry, He never took a wife, despite what some Gnostic texts and modern writers might say. However, it must be noted that Jesus is called the Bridegroom of the Church (Matthew 9:15 and Revelation 21:2). So, this doesn't really apply as much.

All of these examples show how powerful a Christian can be during their singlehood.

About Being Single

One day, I was at a 24-hour diner with Matt. We just came from a short film screening from an art college, where he taught. It was close to midnight. As it started to rain outside, I realized something.

"You know Matt," I said. "When we get married, we won't be able to do things like this any more."

Matt paused, like a deer in headlights.

"When we get wives, we won't be able to hang out like this any more," I clarified. "We will need to be with our wives and families. We will still hang out. But, it won't be the same."

Matt thought my sudden statement was prophetic. However, I think it was sheer common sense. When I get married, I will not be able to do the same things I did while I was single.

Being single, I do have a little bit of advice.

First and foremost, do not set your mind on fleshly things (Romans 8:5-8). This includes not looking at pornography. Many singles struggle with pornography, as they do not have a spouse yet.

"We make our situation as a single incredibly more difficult by doing things that set our mind and eyes on that," said *Porn-Free*. "Pornography and masturbation are often touted as harmless sexual releases for singles. Far from harmless, porn pieces our minds with evil thoughts, while masturbation reinforces the addictive thought patterns."

Second, we must also ask God for provision. If you want to marry, ask God for a spouse who is fit for you. When Adam was created, the Lord saw Adam's need for a companion. The Lord said in Genesis 2:18, *"[It is] not good that man should be alone; I will make him a helper comparable to him."* Accordingly, we must not want a spouse just for our own lustful pleasures (James 4:2,3). We must ask according to the Lord's will, and with obedience.

Third, we must use singlehood as a time to seek God. Similarly, we must use this time to ask God to prepare us for a spouse. Matthew 6:33 says, *seek first the kingdom of God and His righteousness, and all these things shall be added to you.*

Note that we must seek His righteousness as well. Too many Christians are so adamant to be rid of singlehood. But, they are unwilling to take a step back and look at themselves honestly. In other words, the Christian single may not see things in themselves that need to be worked out before marriage.

Singlehood must be used as a time of spiritual growth, not complaining about being alone. Instead of complaining, we can be doing other things of some kind of worth. I myself do not want to look back and see that I have wasted my singlehood on frivolous things.

Finally, we must not be concerned about other people's situations. "It is so easy to look around and wonder why God blessed other people and not you," *Porn-Free* said. "Keep in mind that you are specially designed and unique…Their situations and purposes in life are different from yours (Cook)."

I can look around and wonder why God hasn't sent me anyone yet, while others do have a mate. But we shouldn't be envious or jealous of these people. For one, they might not even be in a relationship the Lord ordained. Second, each one of us has a different life. Who knows what the Lord will do in your life if you trust in Him.

Girls that Spontaneously Manifest

During a men's meeting, one of the guys said that we need to aggressively search for a Christian woman to be our wife. In other words, we need to be on the "hunt" for a wife.

"A girl isn't just going to pop out of your Bible!" The guy argued. I must admit, I completely agree with the statement; however, I do not agree with the context. Obviously, a girl isn't going to spontaneously manifest from out the pages of your Bible.

Nevertheless, this is even more reason for the Christian single to be active in the areas God has called them to. This includes both the secular arena as well as the spiritual arena. Obviously, if your Christianity just involves you reading your Bible in your room and not actively engaging the world, then you aren't going to meet anyone.

Out of my eleven years of being saved, I can say that I ran into nine Christian girls who I knew loved the Lord. This is not including girls who were wishy-washy or girls who I met in a fleeting moment. Someone may ask, "Well, why aren't any of them my wife?" Well, because I wasn't ready to take on a wife, nor were any of these women called to be my wife.

I met all of these girls in the context of doing what God has called me to do. When I was forming a Bible club in high school, I met some Christian girls. When I was witnessing and hanging out at my community college, I ran into them. I met some while hanging out at a friend's Christian college. I even ran into a strong Christian girl when I went to journalism camp at a secular college downstate!

I did none of these things with the *intent* to find a Christian wife. I was where God placed me. You will run into people. You add all this up with God's providence, and you can see why it's not hard to believe that God will provide for you.

I am not trying to be logical about this. I am not trying to calculate up how many Christian girls a male believer will run into during his walk. But I am trying to encourage Christian singles to use their singlehood. Singlehood is not some kind of punishment. Singlehood is a chance to seek after God unhindered. Singlehood, as well as marriage, is a blessing.

Chapter 9 – Dating

I must admit that out of all the chapters I wrote, this one intrigued me the most. If I want to get married, then I need to date a person first, right? Right?

In this chapter, we will also look at dating, as well as Christian dating sites. After looking at Scripture and some tips, we will see if there is an alternative to dating.

Christian Internet Dating

There are literally hundreds of dating sites out there, many of which cater to the Christian crowd.

I went to Christiansingles.com for data. When I first went back, years ago, it was closed. However, three years later, another Christian dating company bought the domain.

Big House (bighouse.com) was another Christian dating site I analyzed. As of the second draft of this book, *Big House* has closed down. It seems sites like this don't last very long. The domain has not yet been used for something else. Nonetheless, when I first started writing this book, I printed off a few pages for future reference.

The tagline was *'Bringing people together in love and faith'*. Immediately, I see pictures of six attractive people on the homepage. A big button laid on that page, with the words 'JOIN for FREE' imprinted on it. On the bottom of the page, the verse Genesis 2:24 is cited in smaller letters.

The registration page asks the user to give their personal information, including what kind of relationship they are seeking, how serious they are with God, and your denomination.

The help section describes the purpose of Bighouse.com as a tool for relationship connections. You can *'find exactly the kind of person you are looking for'*, whether it be dating, or *'a variety of encounters'*. There are tips in the articles how to break up and how to say, No.

There are other sites that are devoted to hooking up Christian singles, such as *Christian Mingle*. I honestly believe some really want to help young believers find their partner.

However, I felt an underlying current of anxiety with Christian dating sites in general. There is an emphasis on finding your soul mate *now*. On top of that, the Christian and the site's system are in control. I sensed some human striving, no matter how hard these sites Christianize their system.

The appeal of these sites is that the user has control. Also, the sites fulfill the desire to be with someone (or at least, they try). I wonder how many users of these Christian dating sites dislike the program. With digital surveys meant to give the believer what they want, one element is ambiguous: God Himself.

Overall, I get the impression that Christian dating sites discourage waiting on the Lord. Instead, they seem to encourage disbelief in God's providence.

Am I completely condemning Christians who used these sites, and found happy marriages? No, not really. I am simply troubled, though, and I believe for good reasons. Just a quick look through these profiles makes me wonder about the heart state of the users. Doesn't it seem a little desperate?

Friendship

I always thought that when I found my wife, there would be a godly friendship there first. So, because friendship is often a preliminary before dating and marriage, we will cover a few verses on friendship.

True friends will correct you. Proverbs 27:5,6 says, *open rebuke [is] better than love carefully concealed. Faithful [are] the wounds of a friend, but the kisses of an enemy [are] deceitful.*

One key mark of friendship is honesty. If you truly love someone, you will tell him or her the truth, even if it isn't the most joyful thing. Obviously, we are not supposed to be needlessly harsh.

However, enablement is a form of hatred. Verse 6 says that the kisses of an enemy are deceitful.

Proverbs 27:17 says, *[as] iron sharpens iron, so a man sharpens the countenance of his friend.* A Christian being sharpened by another Christian marks godly friendship. In other words, they help each other's spiritual growth and walk. Note that this doesn't mean that friends are exactly alike. In fact, differences can help foster deeper friendships.

We should strive for friendships that sharpen our Christian walk. Let us not just befriend someone who is nice, but will challenge us if need be.

Likewise, friends help each other spiritually.

Ecclesiastes 4:9-12 says,

9. Two [are] better than one, because they have a good reward for their labor. 10. For if they fall, one will lift up his companion. But woe to him [who is] alone when he falls, for [he has] no one to help him up. 11. Again, if two lie down together, they will keep warm; But how can one be warm [alone]? 12. Though one may be overpowered by another, two can withstand him. And a threefold cord is not quickly broken.

It always helps to have friends, especially when you fall. Friends can pray for you, as well as simply be there.

In the context of marriage, a Christian can help in many ways. One of the things that came up prominently in the interviews of married couples was the ability to pray with one's spouse. If a premarital relationship isn't causing you to walk closer with God, then it must be brought under consideration. If a relationship is causing you to fall away from God, then it must be cut off.

Acts 2:42-47 says,

42. And they continued steadfastly in the apostles' doctrine and fellowship, in the breaking of bread, and in prayers. 43. Then fear came upon every soul, and many wonders and signs were done through the apostles. 44. Now all who believed were together, and had all things in common, 45. and sold their possessions and goods, and divided them among all, as anyone had need. 46. So continuing daily with one accord in the temple, and breaking bread from house to house, they ate their food with gladness and simplicity of heart, 47. praising God and having favor with all the people. And the Lord added to the church daily those who were being saved.

Christian friendships have the call of Jesus as their goal, and not selfish ambition. Verse 42 says they continued in fellowship. Verse 44 says that early Christians shared things with one another, whether it was their money or possessions.

Verse 46 says they broke bread together. The focus wasn't necessarily the eating. The focus was that they ate from *house to house* and *with gladness*. They went under each other's roofs and enjoyed each other's presence. The focus was God being among them (Matthew 18:20).

Verse 47 talks about praising God. We can see that God was in their conversations, and not just idle talk. If Jesus is not the focus of our speech in Christian friendships, then what is the objective of the relationship?

Dating or Courting?

Dating has its snares, even when Internet matchmakers aren't involved. Usually, dating starts when either a man or woman starts a relationship that is more than just a friendship. Usually, there is no supervision and marriage may or may not be the intent.

"I grew up with the mentality that a lot of us do, having a girlfriend (or boyfriend, in a girl's case) is a nutritious part of this complete teenage experience," said Joshua Harris in a message called *Dating: God's Way*. Harris is renown for his writing on relationships within the body of Christ. "And yet, I've made a decision not to date, not to be pursuing short-term romance with anyone, waiting until I am ready for marriage to get anything stated beyond friendship with girls."

Friendship? But there has to be some kind of bridge between friendship and marriage. One alternative to dating is courting.

A reader may ask, "Courting? How is that any different than dating? It is practically the same thing."

However, there is a difference.

Courtship starts when a single man approaches a single woman by going through the woman's father. A relationship begins under the oversight of the woman's father, family or church. Courtship keeps marriage as its end.

This is not to say that dating is inherently evil. As Joshua Harris notes in his book, *I Kissed Dating Goodbye*, a "serial courter" can live completely like the world. Likewise, a "saintly dater" can be guided by holiness and purity (Harris). In reality, the method isn't as important as the state of the heart.

Scott Croft, an elder of Capitol Hill Baptist Church, teaches Courtship & Dating CORE seminar. Croft named three main differences. The first and foremost is the man's motive in the relationship. A man courts a woman because he believes that woman could be his wife. This applies to "saintly" dating as well.

Second, there is a difference in the mindset of the couple's dealings with one another. Modern dating tends to lean more towards selfishness.

"I do not mean maliciously selfish, as in "I'm going to try to hurt you for my benefit."" Croft wrote. "I mean an oblivious self-centeredness that treats the whole process as ultimately about *me* (Croft)."

The focus of many modern relationships is on what the person wants for him or herself. A majority of the focus tends to be placed on looks, the opinion of friends and self-fulfillment.

No relationship should be based on selfishness. Ephesians 5:25 states that the role of a married man is to be sacrificial. Philippians 2:3 says, *let nothing be done through selfish ambition or conceit, but in lowliness of mind let each esteem others better than himself.*

The focus is no longer on what you want, but on what the other person needs. As Christians, we must ask ourselves, "How can I be the one for her (or him)?"

Finally, there is a difference in methods. In modern dating, intimacy usually precedes commitment. In courtship, there is commitment before intimacy.

"According to the current school of thought, the best way to figure out whether you want to marry a particular person is to act as if you are married and see if you like it," Croft wrote. "Spend large amounts of time alone together. Become each other's primary emotional confidants. Share your deepest secrets and desires. Get to know that person better than anyone else in your life."

In modern premarital relationships, physical intimacy and intensity grow at the same rate as emotional intimacy. The relationship is normally private and, as a result, no one is accountable to an authority.

Physical and emotional intimacy without commitment is clearly damaging. A man may give the impression of a marriage-like position to a woman where there is none; this is deception. Giving a false impression to a sister in Christ violates 1 Thessalonians 4:6. Croft notes that this vague position is cruel to the very woman the man claims to care about.

"The man should show leadership and willingness to bear the risk of rejection by defining the nature and the pace of the relationship," Croft wrote. "He should do this before spending significant time alone with her in order to avoid hurting or confusing her."

When a couple courts, they should seek time with married couples and friends, not just being by themselves. The conversations should never reach the point where one defrauds one another. There should be no physical intimacy outside the bonds of marriage (Hebrews 13:4).

"Within this model, both parties should seek to find out, before God, whether they should be married, and whether they can service and honor God better together than apart," Croft wrote. "The man should take care not to treat any woman like his wife who is not his wife."

And as Elizabeth Elliot said in *Passion and Purity*, "Unless a man is prepared to ask a woman to be his wife, what right has he to claim her exclusive attention?"

Pseudo-Marriage

Modern dating can sometimes become, as Croft wrote, a *pseudo-marriage*. If it works, then real marriage comes. If it doesn't, then let the painful chips fall where they may.

"What we've done is sort of inserted a new category of relationships," Harris said. "Instead of being single with no commitment or married in a life-long commitment, we are in short-term relationship. A relationship that is really for the sake of the relationship."

The Bible always references premarital relationships in the act of men marrying and women being given in marriage (Matthew 24:38 and Luke 20:34,35). Numbers 30:3-16 speaks of the shift of authority from father to husband, when the woman leaves her father and unites with her husband. Song of Solomon showcases the meeting, courtship, and marriage of a couple. These passages do not suggest or argue that marriage is the end of these relationships. They assume marriage is the goal.

Does the Bible offer any other view? No, recreational dating (or dating just for the sake of dating) is never shown in the Bible.

"The category of premarital intimacy does not exist, other than in the context of grievous sexual sin," Croft writes. "The motive for dating or courting is marriage. The practical advice I give the singles at our church is, if you cannot happily see yourself as a married man (or woman) in less than one year, then you are not ready to date."

Is it possible that courtship isn't popular due to the fact that it involves an authority over the relationship? Remember that I am referring to popularity within the Christian Church and not unbelievers. Without any oversight, modern dating can tend to lead in any direction, good or bad.

I am not saying everyone needs an arranged marriage. And, if a believer's heart isn't right, courting can go south as well. However, the safeguard of courtship has been lost. Whatever method we choose, if we desire God's best, we need to follow God's ways.

Chapter 10 – Waiting

Waiting on the Lord is crucial if you want to get anything good. As the old cliché goes, good things come to those who wait. This is especially important for Christians who are single and desire to have a mate.

Waiting isn't easy though. I can testify to that. It becomes even harder when peers compromise their beliefs for an ungodly relationship. Nevertheless, one of the most important things that the Lord calls us to be patient for is his provision for a spouse.

During the interview with my pastor and his wife, Pastor Mike said that patience would always be a very typical fruit of true love. Even when he first met his wife Ana, he recalled, there was a very odd peace and lack of anxiety about the relationship (despite the improbability of seeing Ana again). Everything else before he met his wife was infatuative and hurried.

"With Ana, it was the opposite, I was just comfortable with whatever would happen," Pastor Mike said. "And for me to be alright like that with no concern, I thought that was patience."

Pastor Mike noted that patience almost always has to be in a godly union. If heavy impatience occurs, that might be a red flag that something is wrong.

"It doesn't automatically say it's not God," Pastor Mike

continued. "Maybe your flesh gets in the way. But, I would say that the lack of patience should give you a bit of pause."

"Patience is knowing that what God said is, and will be done in His time," Ana, Pastor Mike's wife, said. "And if you are a believer, and you believe that what God speaks is true, you don't have to lean on your understanding and your own knowledge of trying to make something there."

Jacob and Rachel

Pastor Mike brought up something important one time I had lunch with him. He talked about the story of Jacob and how he waited for Rachel seven years.

Genesis 29:14-20 says,

14. And Laban said to him, "Surely you [are] my bone and my flesh." And he stayed with him for a month. 15. Then Laban said to Jacob, "Because you [are] my relative, should you therefore serve me for nothing? Tell me, what [should] your wages [be]?" 16. Now Laban had two daughters: the name of the elder [was] Leah, and the name of the younger [was] Rachel. 17. Leah's eyes [were] delicate, but Rachel was beautiful of form and appearance. 18. Now Jacob loved Rachel; so he said, "I will serve you seven years for Rachel your younger daughter." 19. And Laban said, "[It is] better that I give her to you than that I should give her to another man. Stay with me." 20. So Jacob served seven years for Rachel, and they seemed [only] a few days to him because of the love he had for her.

Jacob was fleeing from his brother Esau. As Jacob fled, he ran into the daughter and sheep of uncle Laban. In the eyes of Jacob and many other men of the time, Rachel was beautiful.

Note how long Jacob waited to actually be with her. Jacob was willing to wait for Rachel seven years. Today, some believers may say that love can't wait. Nevertheless, Jacob's love for Rachel actually made the wait effortless.

One reason this seven-year wait felt momentary was because he worked towards being with her. In other words, Jacob was *doing* something during this period of waiting, instead of remaining idle.

Also, Jacob's love for Rachel gave him the ability to wait. This is including the next seven years, after Laban tricked Jacob with Leah (Genesis 29:24-28). Thus, Jacob waited a total of fourteen years to be with the one he loved.

Most in the modern Church are not willing to wait a week to be with someone. The impatient believer may equate waiting with hesitation, disbelief, or low self-esteem. Nevertheless, Jacob's patience actually shows true love.

Patience

We need patience. And not just in dating and relationships, but in every area of life.

The American culture does not help with this. We are used to quick media clips or fast one-liners. The American culture does not tolerate slowing down and reflecting. The lack of patience is one reason missionary dating thrives. Impatience shows a lack of trust in God. As discussed in Chapter 3, impatience in relationships can cause the compromised Christian to go seeking in the world. There are many verses on patience; however, we will only discuss two.

Romans 15:4-5 says,

4. For whatever things were written before were written for our learning, that we through the patience and comfort of the Scriptures might have hope. 5. Now may the God of patience and comfort grant you to be like-minded toward one another, according to Christ Jesus,

The things written in the Old Testament were written so that we might have patience. A major example of this includes the whole book of Job (James 5:11). Notice how Paul intertwines patience with comfort and hope. We are patient because we have hope, and there is comfort in patience. Also, verse 5 says that the Lord is the God of Patience. Since He is longsuffering with us, we also ought to be longsuffering one towards another.

James 1:2-4 says,

2. My brethren, count it all joy when you fall into various trials, 3. knowing that the testing of your faith produces patience. 4. But let patience have [its] perfect work, that you may be perfect and complete, lacking nothing.

This speaks of patience in the context of trials. However, the waiting for a spouse can be counted as a trial. The waiting for a spouse tests the faith. Those who lack faith may go to the world. However, those who count the trial as joy will gain patience.

When we are patient, God's perfect work is achieved in us. We may think that we lack when we don't have what we want. But, verse 4 says that we lack nothing when we are patient. Therefore, you can see a bit of an irony. When we are impatient, and try to get something on our own strength, we become incomplete. This can include the context of missionary dating being "successful". However, if we are patient on God, we become complete. We become God's perfect work, though we may appear to be lacking. This can include the period of waiting for a spouse.

Waiting on God

Psalm 27:14 says, *wait on the Lord; be of good courage, and He shall strengthen your heart; wait, I say, on the Lord!* When I say wait on the Lord, some Christians think I mean doing nothing. Remember the

Christian at the end of Chapter 8? He equated waiting on the Lord with girls spontaneously popping out of Bibles.

These kinds of statements reveal the impatient heart. Waiting is not passive in the sense that you are doing nothing. As we are waiting, we are praying, witnessing to the world, and getting to know the Lord better. In other words, the patient Christian is involved in an active waiting. As it says in the Scriptures, seek first the kingdom of God, and all things will be added (Matthew 6:33).

Seeking the kingdom to the impatient Christian is nothing, though. When Christians hold this attitude, it's easy to see why things like *Big House* become so popular. This is because there is a lack of faith and patience to begin with.

Psalm 62:5-8 says,

5. My soul, wait silently for God alone, for my expectation [is] from Him. 6. He only [is] my rock and my salvation; [He is] my defense; I shall not be moved. 7. In God [is] my salvation and my glory; the rock of my strength, [and] my refuge, [is] in God. 8. Trust in Him at all times, you people; pour out your heart before Him; God [is] a refuge for us. Selah

Verse 5 says to wait silently. In other words, don't be complaining as you are waiting. If you are waiting for a spouse, and complaining about God's plan, your "patience" is not producing faith.

Verses 6-7 repeats that God is the only rock and salvation. In the context of waiting for a spouse, remember that God is our only salvation, not another person. Don't expect that other person (when they come) will have the ability to change anything in you. Only God can do that.

Verse 8 is related to waiting, as waiting requires trusting in the Lord at all times. Verse 8 also says that, as we trust in Him, we must pour out our heart before Him. God is not far off from our distress. God is waiting for us to pour our hearts out before Him.

Psalm 40:1-4 says,

1. I waited patiently for the Lord; and He inclined to me, and heard my cry. 2. He also brought me up out of a horrible pit, out of the miry clay, and set my feet upon a rock, [and] established my steps. 3. He has put a new song in my mouth-- Praise to our God; many will see [it] and fear, and will trust in the Lord. 4. Blessed [is] that man who makes the Lord his trust, and does not respect the proud, nor such as turn aside to lies.

This is a psalm of David. King David waited patiently on the Lord. When he cried in his waiting, the Lord heard him. Likewise, God is willing to hear our cries and desperation as we wait. Verses 2 and 3 shows the salvation of the Lord, and new life (a new song).

Verse 3 ends with a reaffirmation of trusting in the Lord. Verse 4 says to not trust in the proud or turn aside to lies above trusting in the Lord. Distrusting the Creator involves a kind of pride, in that it says that the compromised Christian knows better than God. Remember, this distrust needs not to be stated, only implied. For example, Christians may endorse missionary dating or Christian dating sites, implying distrust in God.

Finally, Psalm 130:5-6 says, *I wait for the Lord, my soul waits, and in His word I do hope. 6. My soul [waits] for the Lord more than those who watch for the morning-- [yes, more than] those who watch for the morning.*

Psalm 130 is known as De Profundis, or "Out of the Depths I Cried" after the first verse. Again, as in previous psalms we see how waiting is intertwined with crying. When God calls us to wait (especially for a spouse), He is not dismissing our discomfort. Jesus is very familiar with even our smallest distress, as He is called the Man of Sorrows (Isaiah 53:3). Jesus is also known as a High Priest who can sympathize with our weaknesses (Hebrews 4:15).

Contentment

We need to be content where God has placed us. If you are not content being alone, then a relationship will not help.

Philippians 4:6-8 says,

6. Be anxious for nothing, but in everything by prayer and supplication, with thanksgiving, let your requests be made known to God; 7. and the peace of God, which surpasses all understanding, will guard your hearts and minds through Christ Jesus. 8. Finally, brethren, whatever things are true, whatever things [are] noble, whatever things [are] just, whatever things [are] pure, whatever things [are] lovely, whatever things [are] of good report, if [there is] any virtue and if [there is] anything praiseworthy--meditate on these things.

We must not be anxious for anything. This is because God our Father already knows our needs before we ask Him (Matthew 6:8). This includes our need for a spouse. Paul places an alternative to being *anxious*; the alternative is prayer and supplication. Remember that prayer is not just lifting up requests, but also listening for God's voice. *With thanksgiving* reminds the prayerful Christian to be mindful of what God already has given to them.

Paul encourages the Philippians to let their requests be known to God. There is nothing wrong with asking God for something. However, it must be according to His will (1 John 5:14).

Verse 8 lists the things a Christian needs to think about. Many times, Christians will focus on that which they don't have. I do not mean that a person should be delusional. Yet, our lack must be put into the greater context of God's will.

In the next verses, Paul speaks about what needs to be done when we are in need.

Philippians 4:9-13 says,

9. The things which you learned and received and heard and saw in me, these do, and the God of peace will be with you. 10. But I rejoiced in the Lord greatly that now at last your care for me has flourished again; though you surely did care, but you lacked opportunity. 11. Not that I speak in regard to need, for I have learned in whatever state I am, to be content: 12. I know how to be abased, and I know how to abound. Everywhere and in all things I have learned both to be full and to be hungry, both to abound and to suffer need. 13. I can do all things through Christ who strengthens me.

Again, verse 9 calls the Lord the God of Peace, similar to the peace of God in verse 7. Again, peace comes when we wait on the Lord. Keep in mind, this is a supernatural peace that is not based on logic. It is a peace that comes when there should be no peace.

Verse 10 speaks of how the Philippians cared for Paul. However, Paul begins writing specifically in regard to need in verse 11. Thus, Paul says that whatever state he is in, he learned how to be content. We need to learn how to be content.

Verse 12 speaks about how to suffer. When we suffer, we normally don't think about how there is a certain way to suffer. Modern Christians don't want to suffer any kind of discontent at all. In the context of relationships, many Christians are willing to compromise their walk to eliminate the discontent of loneliness.

Verse 13 brings up a popular verse, though it is popular for being placed out of context. *I can do all things through Christ who strengthens me* does not necessarily refer to material success.

In context, you can see that God gives us the strength to be content under suffering or strain. In the context of singlehood, God gives us the strength to wait for a spouse.

Our contentment needs to be in God alone, and not another person. People will fail us, but God never fails us. Many times I hear Christian guys say that if they get married, then everything will be perfect. However, a broken person cannot completely fulfill the needs of another broken person. And we all are broken.

Chapter 11 – Advice from the Married

Marriage is truly a beautiful thing.

"Marriage is an exclusive union between one man and one woman, publicly acknowledged, permanently sealed, and physically consummated," said Selwyn Hughes, a Welsh Christian minister known for writing *Every Day with Jesus*.

In the modern world, marriage is no longer treated like something sacred. It is instead replaced by cohabitation and loose sexual encounters. Though the world may change, the Word of God stands true.

In my revising of the *Guide*, I discovered I needed one more interview. After all, out of all the chapters, this is the one I am unable to give personal testimony on (since I am single as of the writing of this book). I sought several married couples to get an interview before my personal deadline. Some couples never responded; tragedy hit other couples. I discussed the matter with my pastor. He asked if I thought about interviewing my parents for the book.

I said I did. However, the thought of it made me a bit uneasy. I believe that it is sometimes difficult for any child to ask a parent for relational advice, let alone an interview for a book.

However, after thinking about it, the closeness of including my own parents might be just what this book needed.

Interview: The Azamars

My parents, Julio and Gloria Azamar, met at a department store called Zayre. My father bought some automotive products, and my mother was a clerk. My father went to purchase the product, and started talking to her. He asked for her number, and eventually they started dating. At that time, neither of my parents attended church.

My parents were married 26 years ago (about a year before I was born). My parents have both rededicated themselves to the Lord since then. In the beginning of the relationship, there were some financial difficulties. However, God helped them through it. I asked my parents about marriage, divorce and relationships in general.

"Marriage in the Bible is a union that represents companionship, love, patience, understanding, kindness and generosity," my Dad said. "All of these things should come out in the relationship when you get married. Sometimes we think of the sacrifice as very great. But, the Bible says that true love is sacrifice. And that's why when we say we love somebody else, we should be willing to sacrifice and be willing to show it."

My Dad related the sacrificial nature of love to how God sent His Son as a sacrifice for our sins. He noted that it is a very difficult thing for us to do, since sacrifice goes against our sinful nature.

My Mom said that we as human beings naturally desire companionship. It helps us grow in our understanding of each other and God Himself. When asked about certain good traits a Christian man should look for in a wife, she included a respect for neighbors and responsibility. My mother also said that the way the woman treats her parents should be observed.

"I believe that if that young lady is going to respect her father, she is going to be able to respect her husband," she said. "I think that establishes it really well; like how a young man treats his mother."

When asked about the high divorce rate in the Church, my Dad said that although a lot of people go to local congregation, they don't adhere to scriptural teachings. In other words, many Christians conduct their lives just like the world.

"The Church is suppose to be separate from the world," my mother said, following the question on divorce. "You are supposed to be able to walk into the church, and see those differences. Why is it you go into a church, and you find a man and a woman together; but, you find out later they are not married? But I never understood how can you be a Christian and get a divorce. Maybe it was unequally yoked to begin with; God may have not brought that together."

My Dad described marriage as God's way of teaching us how to apply teachings to others, because that is the most intimate relationship you can have.

"That is how we learn," he said. "That is how we grow, and how we learn about ourselves, and how we learn about others."

My father believes that everyone (himself included) comes into marriage with preconceived notions. We normally expect a person to be a certain way, and it usually ends up that the person and the relationship is not what we expect it to be.

"But, God allows that to happen for us to grow, because we usually only grow through adversity. When things are going fine and smooth, we usually don't grow," my Dad said. "We usually have to have some kind of difficulty or trial and that's usually what allows us to grow in our faith and understanding of God's will."

My father said at the beginning of the marriage, he didn't ascribe to any Christian values, since he was living in the world. But now he believes that the Scriptures tell us how to conduct our relationships, including marriage. My Dad said that the media and the world give a superficial image of love. A lot of people are misguided even in the body of Christ.

"Sometimes, people just want to get married because they are lonely, not because they are seeking to establish a long-term relationship," my father said. "A lot of times people get married for physical looks. A lot of times people get married for money. All of those superficial things make it harder for a marriage; you have to have much deeper reasons for being married, because that is the only way to stay married and uphold the commitment."

In addition, my Dad noted that the temptations of men are

generally physical in nature. Men are generally tempted by what they see. My mother noted that women deal with the desire to be attractive to man. She said that many women risk their health to become physically attractive. I was reminded about something another person said: Men lust, and women want to be lusted after.

I asked my parents if they had any advice for young Christian men and women who would read the *Guide*. My Dad said no matter what kind of trials and temptations the reader may encounter, if you truly want to be blessed, the word of God must be adhered to.

"No matter how you get tempted to get sidetracked by the world and all its little and big things that attack you, go to God," my father said. "And let God, through the Holy Spirit and Word direct your paths."

My Mom said that young Christian women can still enjoy living in this world, but it must all be done within the confines of the Bible. She said Christian women need to be strong and straight to the point. However, she also said that a woman who talks too much and is too loud could be unladylike. She clarified that there needs to be a balance. The truth, she said, is going to speak loud enough.

"A Christian woman shouldn't be out all hours of the night wearing scantily clothes," my mother said. "That's not what I am talking about. She should have some kind of standards for herself that are going to reflect that she is a Christian woman."

"I believe that marriage, because it is ordained by God, is a beautiful thing," my Dad said. "It can offer many blessings, which are not just physical, but also spiritual, which are more important. People have to realize that the answer to all of these problems we encounter in life is God."

Reflection of a Mystery

It has been said that the Bible begins and ends with a marriage. The Bible began with the marriage of Adam and Eve, and ends with the Marriage Supper of Christ and His Church. Marriage is a reflection of a great mystery.

Ephesians 5:21-24 says,

21. *submitting to one another in the fear of God. 22. Wives, submit to your own husbands, as to the Lord. 23. For the husband is head of the wife, as also Christ is head of the church; and He is the Savior of the body. 24 Therefore, just as the church is subject to Christ, so [let] the wives [be] to their own husbands in everything.*

In Chapter 5, Paul addresses how we should walk, as well as the duties of home life and work. Verse 21 says, *submitting to one another.* Wives are called to submit to their husbands. The husband is supposed to be the leader of the wife and the household, as stated in verse 23. The wife is the helpmate of the husband.

This may seem diminutive; however, this is a place of admiration. This submission to the husband reflects the Church's submission to Christ.

The wife's role as a helper isn't always going to be pleasant. Nor, is the husband's role as leader always going to be comfortable. A helper sometimes points out mistakes that are uncomfortable. A leader sometimes needs to make hard decisions.

"Marriage is a refining process," said the Ricuccis from the book *Love that Lasts*. "Conflict will occur in every marriage…The fact is, your spouse won't make you sin. They simply reveal what's already in your heart. One of the best wedding gifts God will give you is a full-length mirror called your spouse. If He were to attach a card it would say, "Here's to helping you discover what you're really like. Congratulations!""

Ephesians 5:25-29 says,

25. Husbands, love your wives, just as Christ also loved the church and gave Himself for her, 26. that He might sanctify and cleanse her with the washing of water by the word, 27. that He might present her to Himself a glorious church, not having spot or wrinkle or any such thing, but that she should be holy and without blemish. 28. So husbands ought to love their own wives as their own bodies; he who loves his wife loves himself. 29. For no one ever hated his own flesh, but nourishes and cherishes it, just as the Lord [does] the church.

Husbands are called to love their wives as Christ loved the Church. A husband's love reflects Christ's love for the Church. It is therefore a sacrificial and unconditional love.

Once, I heard a preacher give two gauges to see if your love for your spouse is true. First, do you love your mate enough that you are willing to die for them? In other words, are you willing to die for them as Christ died for His Church?

Jesus says in John 15:13, *greater love has no one than this, than to lay down one's life for his friends.* Love is sacrificial, and does not require return or repayment. This is in stark contrast to infatuation, which demands reciprocation.

Second, would you love your mate if they were ugly and stinky? When I gave this gauge for a message in my church, everyone broke out laughing. Of course, I'm not promoting bad hygiene. But imagine it: would you still love your prince charming or dream girl if they were physically undesirable? Well, what does that have to do with the love of Christ? Everything.

Our sin is far more detestable to God than any physical fault, such as ugliness and body odor. Yet, while we were yet sinners, Christ died for us (Romans 5:8). Now, I'm no different than anyone else. I would like to have an attractive wife. But, beauty is only skin-deep. In the end, we must unconditionally love, even in the face of adversity and disappointment.

Verses 26 and 27 shows the love of Jesus as well. Jesus cleanses and sanctifies the Church in order to present Himself a church without blemish.

Verse 28 and 29 says that husbands ought to love their own wives as their own bodies, not someone else's wife. Only a lunatic will harm his or her own body. A normal man nourishes himself with food and water. So, husbands are supposed to nourish their wives with spiritual food.

As their own bodies in verse 28 reflects Genesis 2:22-24; the husband and wife are one flesh. Marriage was the first institution ordained by God, even before the government and the Church. "The Bible opens and closes with a wedding," said Selwyn Hughes, referencing the Marriage Supper of the Lamb (Revelation 19:7-10).

Ephesians 5:30-33 says,

30. For we are members of His body, of His flesh and of His bones. 31. "For this reason a man shall leave his father and mother and be joined to his wife, and the two shall become one flesh." 32. This is a great mystery, but I speak concerning Christ and the church. 33. Nevertheless let each one of you in particular so love his own wife as himself, and let the wife [see] that she respects [her] husband.

Verse 30 says we are members of the body of Christ. Verse 31 relates how husband and wife are one flesh once again. At the end of the chapter, Paul brings the reader back, telling the husbands to love their wives and wives to respect their husbands. Similarly, Colossians 3:18-19 says, *wives, submit yourselves unto your own husbands, as it is fit in the Lord. Husbands, love your wives, and be not bitter against them.*

The relationship of Christ and His Church is a great mystery. It is beyond our understanding. Earthly marriage is a shadow of this relationship between God and His People. Consequently, marriage must not be taken lightly.

Self-Control and Sexuality

Even among some Christians, unconscious selfishness blurs the purpose of marriage. 1 Corinthians 7:1-6 says,

1. Now concerning the things of which you wrote to me: [It is] good for a man not to touch a woman. 2. Nevertheless, because of sexual immorality, let each man have his own wife, and let each woman have her own husband. 3. Let the husband render to his wife the affection due her, and likewise also the wife to her husband. 4. The wife does not have authority over her own body, but the husband [does]. And likewise the husband does not have authority over his own body, but the wife [does]. 5. Do not deprive one another except with consent for a time, that you may give yourselves to fasting and prayer; and come together again so that Satan does not tempt you because of your lack of self-control. 6. But I say this as a concession, not as a commandment.

It is not good for a man to touch a woman if they are unmarried. This includes "innocent" things like making out. Of course, I am not saying that kissing is equivalent to fornication. However, young Christians need to be careful about what they do. One of my interviewees noted how kissing can incite lustful desires.

Unfortunately, the modern Church takes it way beyond just kissing.

Because of sexual immorality, as stated in verse 2, the Lord permits marriage. The husband and wife are told to foster mutual respect for one another. With respect, the wife is to "control" the body of her husband, and visa versa. Notice how control of the body is transferred from self, and placed in the hands of the other mate.

Paul tells the married couple to not deprive themselves of intercourse; unless it is for prayer and fasting. Physical desires (eating, sexuality) can be put on hold for a season. However, the marriage bed is set as a safety guard against temptation. This is not a commandment, as stated in verse 6. In other words, the married couple holds the freedom of when and when not to deny their desires for fasting and prayer.

1 Corinthians 7:7-11 says,

7. For I wish that all men were even as I myself. But each one has his own gift from God, one in this manner and another in that. 8. But I say to the unmarried and to the widows: It is good for them if they remain even as I am; 9. but if they cannot exercise self-control, let them marry. For it is better to marry than to burn [with passion]. 10. Now to the married I command, [yet] not I but the Lord: A wife is not to depart from [her] husband.11. But even if she does depart, let her remain unmarried or be reconciled to [her] husband. And a husband is not to divorce [his] wife.

Paul says in verse 7 that he desires all men to be as he is: single. This even goes back to Chapter 8, where I discussed the freedom of singlehood. Singles have ability to get things done differently than a married person. Nevertheless, every *man has his own gift from God*. On that note, believers need to seek out the Lord's will for their life, whether it is to marry or remain single. Verse 8 says it is good for the unmarried to remain unmarried, if they can control themselves. However, if there is a lack of self-control, then marriage is better. It is better to marry then to burn with lustful passions (verse 9).

Verse 10 affirms that a wife should not depart from her husband. Unlike previous verses stating that marriage is the choice of the believer, *staying* in a marriage is not optional. Marriage is supposed to be permanent. Whereas the option of singlehood is from Paul, staying married is from the Lord.

Verse 11 says that if the wife does depart there are two options. These can be applied to the husband as well. First is reconciliation. Second is for her to remain unmarried. More of this will be discussed in the next chapter.

Salvation after Marriage

But what happens when one spouse accepts the Lord, and the other does not? For example, there is a lost couple where neither person is saved. The wife hears the Gospel and becomes a Christian. However, the husband does not. This can occur the other way as well, with the husband accepting Christ. So what does the believing spouse do? Amazingly, the Lord through Paul gives us an answer. Since Corinthians is a major part of this chapter, this seems like the best place to address this.

1 Corinthians 7:12-14 says,

12. But to the rest I, not the Lord, say: If any brother has a wife who does not believe, and she is willing to live with him, let him not divorce her. 13. And a woman who has a husband who does not believe, if he is willing to live with her, let her not divorce him. 14. For the unbelieving husband is sanctified by the wife, and the unbelieving wife is sanctified by the husband; otherwise your children would be unclean, but now they are holy.

Note how Paul says that this is from him, not the Lord. Again, this is not a commandment. If any brother in the faith has an unbelieving wife that is compliant to live with, then divorce isn't an option. This addresses believers who marry after salvation. This verse does not justify missionary dating. Verse 13 shows this goes for the Christian wife as well.

In verse 14, we see that the believer sanctifies the children and unbeliever.

1 Corinthians 7:15-17 says,

15. But if the unbeliever departs, let him depart; a brother or a sister is not under bondage in such [cases]. But God has called us to peace. 16. For how do you know, O wife, whether you will save [your] husband? Or how do you know,

O husband, whether you will save [your] wife? 17. But as God has distributed to each one, as the Lord has called each one, so let him walk. And so I ordain in all the churches.

Verse 15 constitutes abandonment, one of the few justifications for divorce besides adultery and physical abuse. Abandonment will be discussed in depth in the next chapter.

If the unbeliever physically departs, let them depart. The believer is not under bondage if this happens. And what is bondage? The bondage often associated with unrighteous divorce. Nevertheless, the Lord called us to peace.

Verse 16 says that the unbeliever might be saved through the providence of God. Believers are called to remain with the unbelievers in marriage.

And in verse 17, God's providence is shown in His distribution of His children. In whatever state God has called you in (whether single or married) let the Christian walk in that state with righteousness.

Chapter 12 – A Lack of Commitment

Till death do us part has been eroded to *Till annoyances do us part*. Just look at the divorce rates. As of 2008, 46% of all marriages involve remarriage for one or both spouses; nearly 40% of all marriages end in divorce in the United States (Sratling).

The scary thing is that there is no difference in the Christian Church. I say this with as much love as possible. I also say this with all humility, as I am part of the body of Christ. This is especially true since I see firsthand the effects of divorce on my friends. Aren't the people of God supposed to be an example? Why are we not being a light?

During the interview with my pastor and his wife, Pastor Mike made an interesting comment about why the divorce rate is so high within the Church. He believes it is a side effect of half-hearted commitments to God the Father.

"Mankind is losing his ability to be wholly committed to God," Pastor Mike said. "The adultery rate spiritually to the Father is at an all time high. And whenever the relationship with God is defiled and the standard of that relationship is lowered, the shadow of it (marriage) is absolutely going to hurt."

Pastor Mike also noted how he has seen many spouses offer roughly the same amount of devotion to their mate that they would give to God. In other words, they give to their mate about what they are giving to God.

"There is not a big discrepancy between them cheating on God and them cheating on their mate," Pastor Mike said.

Because of the Hardness of Hearts

One thing must be remembered as we continue into this chapter on divorce: God hates it (Malachi 2:16). In this chapter we will address two key Scriptures that deal with divorce. Also, we will give a disturbing example of "emotional" abandonment. Let's look at Scripture.

Deuteronomy 24:1-4 says,

1. "When a man takes a wife and marries her, and it happens that she finds no favor in his eyes because he has found some uncleanness in her, and he writes her a certificate of divorce, puts it in her hand, and sends her out of his house, 2. when she has departed from his house, and goes and becomes another man's wife, 3. if the latter husband detests her and writes her a certificate of divorce, puts it in her hand, and sends her out of his house, or if the latter husband dies who took her as his wife, 4. then her former husband who divorced her must not take her back to be his wife after she has been defiled; for that is an abomination before the Lord, and you shall not bring sin on the land which the Lord your God is giving you as an inheritance.

Divorce is first spoken of in Deuteronomy. It should be noted that during this period, only men are allowed to divorce. However, by the time of the New Testament, women are allowed to file for divorce in the Jewish culture (Mark 10:12).

The "uncleanness" referred to in verse 1 refers to pre-martial sex (1 Corinthians 7:2). Verse 2 shows that the wife can marry again. However, verses 3 and 4 shows that the woman is unable to return to her first husband. The Lord calls this an abomination. Jesus (as he does with other Old Testament laws) clarifies and expands on the laws for divorce.

Matthew 19:3-9 says,

3. The Pharisees also came to Him, testing Him, and saying to Him, "Is it lawful for a man to divorce his wife for [just] any reason?" 4. And He answered and said to them, "Have you not read that He who made [them] at the beginning 'made them male and female,' 5. and said, 'For this reason a man shall leave his father and mother and be joined to his wife, and the two shall become one flesh'? 6. So then, they are no longer two but one flesh. Therefore what God has joined together, let not man separate." 7. They said to Him, "Why then did Moses command to give a certificate of divorce, and to put her away?" 8. He said to them, "Moses, because of the hardness of your hearts, permitted you to divorce your wives, but from the beginning it was not so. 9. And I say to you, whoever divorces his wife, except for sexual immorality, and marries another, commits adultery; and whoever marries her who is divorced commits adultery."

The Pharisees questioned Jesus because they wanted to test Him.

However, this testing of Jesus results in us getting a better view of the Old Testament law on divorce.

The Pharisees ask Jesus if it is lawful to divorce for any reason. Before Jesus gives one of three reasons for divorce, he first addresses the origin of marriage. In verse 4, Jesus states marriage as being established from the beginning. So, it was before any laws were set up for divorce.

In verse 5, Jesus continues to bring the focus back on how God established marriage in the Garden of Eden, as He quotes Genesis 2:22. Marriage is the natural order of God's Creation for mankind. In verse 6, Jesus states that it is an institution of God, as He says what *God has joined together, let not man separate.*

In verse 7, the Pharisees attempt to make Jesus contradict Himself: if God wants people to be married permanently, why did Moses "command" to give a certificate?

In verse 8, Jesus clarifies that divorce was not a command, but a concession. In other words, Moses grudgingly tolerated and permitted divorce. Unlike the concession found in 1 Corinthians 7:6, this one carries more negative connotations. This concession was due to hardness of hearts.

Then, we come to the first of only three conditions in which divorce is allowed. Verse 9 states that if a spouse commits adultery, divorce is permitted. This actually clarifies the "uncleanness" found in Deuteronomy 24:1. If adultery hasn't taken place, and either person chooses to remarry, then they both commit adultery. Also, the person they remarry commits adultery. It should be noted that under the Levitical law and the theocracy of Israel, adultery was punishable by death (Deuteronomy 22:22-24). This shows the gravity of that particular sin.

The second condition that permits divorce is abandonment. Abandonment is defined in terms of a spouse physically leaving the family for a significant amount of time (1 Corinthians 7:15-17). This includes death. A third condition generally accepted is physical abuse. This is common sense, as the spouse's life is in jeopardy. In addition, if the abuser spends time in jail away from the spouse, this falls back into physical abandonment.

However, a new, unscriptural reason for divorce has appeared in recent years. That reason is emotional abandonment.

Interview: Pastor Jay Peters

Jay Peters is the associate pastor for New Life Assembly, a house church in University Park at the time of this writing. He graduated from Christian Life College, and has been involved in ministry for the past 20 years.

Jay has been my youth pastor since my teenage years, and continues to play a major mentorship role in my walk with Christ. I decided to ask for an interview with Jay since he has had several confrontations with Christians attempting to justify unbiblical divorce.

Jay describes divorce as the opposite of what God intended for men and women (Malachi 2:16). When committed outside of biblical boundaries, it is man in his own authority splitting both from his spouse and God's will for marriage (Mark 10-12 and Luke 16:8). He also related this self-authority to the downfall of Israel in the book of Judges, which says *every man did what as right in his own eyes* (Judges 17:6).

Jay describes the effect divorce has on the local body as incredibly destructive. In his 20 years of ministry, Jay has seen collateral damage that continues to this day. This is especially true in a Christian couple, when even those in ministry choose divorce instead of patiently enduring difficult times and trusting God to redeem their marriage.

"I believe that the ultimate purpose in marriage is to make us more like Jesus (Romans 8:29) whereby we become conformed more into His image through the covenant of marriage," Jay said. "This also glorifies God. As Christians are the Bride of Christ, so should marriage reflect the intimate relationship we have with Jesus the Groom. Divorce destroys this witness. The Devil knows this and attacks us and hence there is such widespread divorce in the Church of Jesus Christ today."

As a youth pastor, Jay has seen the devastating affects of divorce falling on the children of couples. God forbids that we cause a little one to stumble because of selfishness (Mark 9:42).

Jay described emotional abandonment as when a spouse is present physically, but no longer expresses interest or concern for the other individual. This is unlike physical abandonment, when the spouse is no longer physically there. An example of emotional abandonment is when a couple no longer speaks to one another, especially in the context of intimate conversation. Another display of emotional abandonment is when spouses no longer sleep in the same bedroom, even while living under the same roof. Often the abandoning spouse will justify their behavior telling others of the negative traits of the spouse. "I just don't feel the love anymore" is a common phrase for the spouses of emotional abandonment.

"Sadly, they often cannot see their own self-absorption and refuse to get help or counsel as they are already convinced in their own mind that there are no other solutions," Jay said.

Emotional abandonment is not justified anywhere in the Scriptures. It isn't even implied as a good reason for divorce. The Bible lays out very simple yet profound truths for marriage. Husbands are told to love their wives as Christ loved the Church in Ephesians 5:25. Wives are told to be submissive to their husbands as is fitting in the Lord in Colossians 3:18. When Christian applies these Scriptures to marriage, it leaves little room for selfishness or emotional abandonment, Jay said.

Jay noted that he rarely has seen biblical reasons for divorce. The common motives have been for selfish reasons, where God was ignored and the Scriptures disregarded.

"One young lady I had counseled with was divorcing her husband because he was 'holding back her potential' in her career as well as her relationship with God," Jay said. "If this was not sad enough, she was told by her own pastor that her reasoning was both just and biblical!"

The young woman explained that divorce became a natural, logical conclusion of an already barren, nonexistent relationship. Her Pastor and elders agreed, stating there were multiple ways to interpret abandonment. The woman described this revelation as a kind of spiritual enlightenment. Jay refuted the woman and the elders, but to no avail.

The road of self preludes Christian couples getting a divorce, says Jay. Self-gratification, self-pity, and self-justification are all foundations for unbiblical divorce.

For Those Struggling

Pastor Jay Peters made one final word for those struggling with divorce.

"For anyone reading these words and struggling with these thoughts, seek God and seek help from an integral pastor or elder in the church," Jay said. "Silence is not golden and often because these things are kept silent for so long, it makes it harder for one to change and restore a relationship."

As Christians, we are called to proclaim a God of love and righteousness. We are called to love one another. How hypocritical and selfish we have become when we cannot keep the vow to love in sickness and in health.

"If this is you, get help now," Jay said. "Don't delay the Spirit of God from working in your marriage and renewing the love and joy that He has always intended for marriage. Remember, God hates divorce!"

Divorce is no longer out of the norm. Because Christians take marriage so lightly, divorce comes as a very easy out. Even in modern Christianity, we've made marriage conditional. In other words, our marital respect becomes based on what the spouse can do for us, instead of sacrificial love.

As stated before, Malachi 2:16 is often quoted in regards to God hating divorce. However, there is deeper meaning to this verse that is often overlooked: Why does God hate divorce?

Malachi 2:15 says, *but did He not make [them] one, having a remnant of the Spirit? And why one? He seeks godly offspring. Therefore take heed to your spirit, and let none deal treacherously with the wife of his youth.*

The Lord says He made them one because He seeks godly offspring. When divorce occurs (especially within the Christian home) it can have a dire effect on the children. Once divorce takes place, selfishness takes over, and the children are caught in the crossfire.

The next chapter will gather info on signs to look for in choosing a spouse, based on Scripture and other biblical sources. In essence, this has been advice given to me for my future. Two passages in Proverbs will be used as the basis of the writings.

Chapter 13 – Proverbs' Guide to Love

And now, for the chapter of this book's namesake.

When I read the Proverbs, I found many insights into relationships and love. During the interview for the *Guide*, my mother reinforced the need to read Proverbs, as it gave much advice for how to respond in many social situations.

In reality, I originally wrote this chapter as an aid for myself. I did not write this chapter as an expert on love. Solomon, the third King of Israel, wrote the majority of the Proverbs. As stated before, the Lord gave him profound wisdom.

Nevertheless, the wisdom of Solomon did not teach him self-control. Many of the Proverbs are for his son, Rehoboam. And though these upcoming verses are addressed to a son, they can be applied to a woman's spiritual walk as well. In spite of the teachings of his father, Rehoboam fell into idolatry, following example rather than words. This eventually led to the division of Israel.

The fool, a reoccurring character in the Proverbs, reflects many of the Solomon's own failures. So, let us not act the part of the fool in our relationships. Let us heed the call to wisdom and godly relationships.

In the Dark Night

Solomon warns his son about evil women throughout the entire book of Proverbs. However, chapter 7 appears to be the most detailed.

Proverbs 7:1-5 says,

1. My son, keep my words, and treasure my commands within you. 2. Keep my commands and live, and my law as the apple of your eye. 3. Bind them on your fingers; write them on the tablet of your heart. 4. Say to wisdom, "You [are] my sister," and call understanding [your] nearest kin, 5. that they may keep you from the immoral woman, from the seductress [who] flatters with her words.

Rehoboam was told to keep his father's commands in his heart. Proverbs 6:23, 24 says, *for the commandment [is] a lamp, and the law a light; reproofs of instruction [are] the way of life, to keep you from the evil woman, from the flattering tongue of a seductress.*

Wisdom and understanding can keep a man from the strange woman and her flattery; however, there must be an application of wisdom. As the life of Solomon proved, just having wisdom isn't good enough. Wisdom is useless if it isn't practiced.

Proverbs 7:6-9 says,

6. For at the window of my house I looked through my lattice, 7. and saw among the simple, I perceived among the youths, a young man devoid of understanding, 8. passing along the street near her corner; and he took the path to her house 9. in the twilight, in the evening, in the black and dark night.

Solomon looked outside his window and noticed a man completely lacking of understanding. Likewise, there are many young men in the Church today that are lacking understanding. Thus, we need to ask the Lord for understanding.

Solomon called this man a simple one. In other words, he called the man unintelligent. This title proves true. What kind of woman does this simple man expect to meet on the street corner at night? Christians know better than to walk the local streets for a relationship, but we may do something subtler. Christians may instead go to places that they shouldn't seeking a relationship. The places can be physical, like a bar or a club. The places can also be spiritual, such as resorting to compromise and unbelief. Either way, Christians often expect to find someone other than what is to be expected in those places.

Also note that this all takes place at night. Night is often used as a cover to do something bad. So you can see that the man intends to do something shameful. The man wants his evil deeds to be hidden from both man and God (John 3:19-21). As we all know, nothing is hidden before God.

Of course, this man runs into someone he would later regret.

Proverbs 7:10-12 says,

10. And there a woman met him, [with] the attire of a harlot, and a crafty heart. 11. She [was] loud and rebellious, her feet would not stay at home. 12. At times [she was] outside, at times in the open square, lurking at every corner.

This woman wears the attire of a harlot. Note that the writer doesn't call her a harlot. But if this woman looks like a harlot, then something is wrong. Likewise, if a person claims to be a Christian, but the fruits show otherwise, something is wrong (Luke 7:17-20).

Verse 11 says she is loud and rebellious. The King James Version translates *rebellious* as *stubborn*. Who wants to be with anyone who doesn't listen well? And who wants to be with a woman who is obnoxious? Proverbs 9:13 says, *a foolish woman is clamorous; [she is] simple, and knows nothing.* We are not talking about a strong woman or an assertive woman. This is more of a contentious assertiveness, as such found in Proverbs 21:19.

Her feet do not remain in her own household. Instead, she is constantly in other people's business. This might also be a reference to her promiscuous nature. Since she is a harlot, she lurks in every corner, seeking men whom she may entangle. Proverbs 23:27, 28 says, *for a harlot [is] a deep pit, and a seductress [is] a narrow well. She also lies in wait as [for] a victim, and increases the unfaithful among men.*

Proverbs 7:13-15 says,

13. So she caught him and kissed him; with an impudent face she said to him: 14. "[I] [have] peace offerings with me; today I have paid my vows. 15. So I came out to meet you, diligently to seek your face, and I have found you.

Again, verse 13, shows her obnoxious and forceful nature. *She grabs the man.* Normally, a man initiates the relationship. The woman also has an impudent face. Impudent means disrespect or presumption.

However, through all her iniquity, this woman has her peace offering, and has paid her vows. There are religious activities occurring, but no true spiritual life in the woman. This is why the Christian must be reliant on God for finding a spouse, whether man or woman. A potential mate may appear religious, however, activity might be hard to distinguish from true love for God, especially if there is an attraction. A love for God is better than religious activity; obedience is better than sacrifice (1 Samuel 15:22).

An Ox to the Slaughter

This woman uses one of the strongest things that can influence a man: flattery. This makes the man feel important and sought after. However, the Lord warns about such empty words (Psalm 12:3).

Proverbs 7:16-17 says, *I have spread my bed with tapestry, colored coverings of Egyptian linen. I have perfumed my bed with myrrh, aloes, and cinnamon.*

This woman is materialistic. She has linen all the way from Egypt. Egypt is sometimes used as a picture for the world in the

Bible. Also compare how this woman has linen from a foreign land, to the Proverbs 31 woman, who makes her own. We will discuss that later.

Besides luxurious items and fragrances, this harlot seems to be physically beautiful. A significant love interest in your life might be beautiful. However, Proverbs 11:22 says, *[as] a ring of gold in a swine's snout, [so is] a lovely woman who lacks discretion.*

Proverbs 7:18-20 says,

18. Come, let us take our fill of love until morning; let us delight ourselves with love. 19. For my husband [is] not at home; he has gone on a long journey; 20. He has taken a bag of money with him, [and] will come home on the appointed day."

Verse 18 sounds good: unlimited "love" until the morning breaks. Many Christians think they can be just as licentious without any consequences. Verse 19 shows this to be adultery. The adulterous woman lacks any conscience. She doesn't see what she is doing as all that bad. Proverbs 30:20 says, *this [is] the way of an adulterous woman: she eats and wipes her mouth, and says, "I have done no wickedness."* In verse 20, the husband is most likely on a business trip (bag of money), ironically providing for the harlot who lives in his house.

The man, once lead by his desire, becomes no smarter than a beast of burden. He becomes an ox to the slaughter.

Proverbs 7:21-23 says,

21. With her enticing speech she caused him to yield, with her flattering lips she seduced him. 22. Immediately he went after her, as an ox goes to the slaughter, or as a fool to the correction of the stocks, 23. Till an arrow struck his liver. As a bird hastens to the snare, He did not know it [would cost] his life.

So this woman can talk really good. With flattery, she can entice a man to do her will. In other words, she's manipulative. Her manipulations lead the man to his death, an unintentional side effect. Ungodly desires leads to sin, which leads to death (James 1:13-15). Verse 23 is often cited as being a sexually transmitted disease. Besides physical sickness, the soul is tainted as well.

Proverbs 7:24-27 says,

24. Now therefore, listen to me, [my] children; Pay attention to the words of my mouth: 25. Do not let your heart turn aside to her ways, Do not stray into her paths; 26. For she has cast down many wounded, and all who were slain by her were strong [men]. 27. Her house [is] the way to hell, Descending to the chambers of death.

Solomon repeats the call to listen, as in the beginning of the Proverb. Why repeat? This is because lust is so deceptive that repetition is needed. Verse 25 tells the reader to not be turned to her ways, or practices.

Verse 26 reminds the readers to not think of themselves so highly as to think they won't fall. After all, this woman has wounded many. Proverbs 6:26 and 27 says, *for by means of a harlot [a man is reduced] to a crust of bread; and an adulteress will prey upon his precious life.*

Can a man take fire to his bosom, and his clothes not be burned? A harlot (and lust in general) can reduce a man to a crust. Can any person play around with sinful desires and not reap some kind of consequence?

The end of such a woman and interaction with such a woman is death and Hell. The significant other doesn't need to be a harlot. Any relationship that isn't based on love and is based on lust can lead to disaster. So we must be watchful and prayerful.

Words of a Mother

At the end of the book of Proverbs, we find a passage different from the passage we just reviewed. King Lemuel wrote this chapter. Even more so, this is a ruler recalling the words of his mother. The identity of King Lemuel remains a mystery. Some say it is a pseudonym of King Solomon. Others say it is an entirely different person. Whoever the king was, the wisdom recorded still applies today.

Proverbs 31:1-3 says,

1. The words of King Lemuel, the utterance which his mother taught him: 2. What, my son? And what, son of my womb? And what, son of my vows? 3. Do not give your strength to women, nor your ways to that which destroys kings.

What I particularly like about this Proverb is that these are the words of a mother to her son. This isn't a man telling another man what to look for in a wife. This mother knows about women from her own experience of being one. The mother exhorts her son to not give his strength to women.

Proverbs 31:4-7 says,

4. [It is] not for kings, O Lemuel, [it is] not for kings to drink wine, nor for princes intoxicating drink; 5. Lest they drink and forget the law, and pervert the justice of all the afflicted. 6. Give strong drink to him who is perishing, and wine to those who are bitter of heart. 7. Let him drink and forget his poverty, and remember his misery no more.

A warning against excessive drinking and alcoholism may seem extraneous to relationships; however, it is important. What kind of spouse drowns himself (or herself) in alcohol? What kind of husband dilutes his anger and frustrations away in liquor? The answer is clear: one who doesn't want to face his problems.

It has been said that if you are angry with someone, take a walk to cool yourself down. However, don't walk to the bar. The solution is to express our difficulties with our partner. The solution is not at the end of a bottle.

Proverbs 31:8-9 says, *open your mouth for the speechless, in the cause of all [who are] appointed to die. Open your mouth, judge righteously, and plead the cause of the poor and needy.*

Once again, the mother of Lemuel defines the role of a man and of a husband. He defends those who cannot defend themselves. He helps the poor and the needy. He judges righteously. This is the role of a man.

Proverbs 31:10-13 says,

10. Who can find a virtuous wife? For her worth [is] far above rubies. 11. The heart of her husband safely trusts her; so he will have no lack of gain. 12. She does him good and not evil all the days of her life. 13. She seeks wool and flax, and willingly works with her hands.

Who can find a virtuous woman? This is the same thing I ask. A virtuous wife can also be translated a *wife of valor*, in the sense of all forms of excellence. In verse 11, the husband is shown to safely trust in her, unlike the harlot of Proverbs 7. The husband does not need to worry about adultery. She will be a helper (Genesis 2:18-20). This woman doesn't fear hard work. She seeks wool and flax. The wife of valor seeks the tools required for her task.

Proverbs 31:14-17 says,

14. She is like the merchant ships, she brings her food from afar. 15. She also rises while it is yet night, and provides food for her household, and a portion for her maidservants. 16. She considers a field and buys it; from her profits she plants a vineyard. 17. She girds herself with strength, and strengthens her arms.

This woman provides for her household, but also for her servants. The wife of valor rises at night, even before the sun rises. In other words, the wife of valor is not lazy.

Note how in verse 16, the virtuous wife considers a field and buys it. She is knowledgeable in business, for she makes a profit. She knows how to handle money. This shows that the virtuous woman is involved in enterprise and entrepreneurship. This puts to shame feminists that argue that the Bible suppresses women. The virtuous woman is assertive and strong, but not obnoxious like the harlot.

Proverbs 31:18-21 says,

18. She perceives that her merchandise [is] good, and her lamp does not go out by night. 19. She stretches out her hands to the distaff, and her hand holds the spindle. 20. She extends her hand to the poor, yes, she reaches out her hands to the needy. 21. She is not afraid of snow for her household, for all her household [is] clothed with scarlet.

Verse 18 shows that the virtuous woman is not only involved in enterprise. She also has an *understanding* of business. She carries an ability to discern if a venture is good or bad.

In verse 19, the virtuous woman stretches her hand to the distaff. A distaff is a tool used for spinning. She also holds her hand to the spindle. Her lamp doesn't go out by night, which means she stays up for work if need be.

The virtuous woman is merciful and compassionate. She extends her hand to the needy and the poor. This merciful nature is most reflected in her relationship with her husband and her children.

Children call her Blessed

My mother has been a blessing to me. She has prayed for me and been a good example of a Christian woman. Proverbs continues to display the advice of a mother.

Proverbs 31:22-24 says,

22. She makes tapestry for herself; her clothing [is] fine linen and purple. 23. Her husband is known in the gates, when he sits among the elders of the land. 24. She makes linen garments and sells [them], and supplies sashes for the merchants.

The virtuous woman makes things with her own hands. In other words, she is productive. This is a stark contrast from the harlot in Proverbs 7:16. The harlot *buys* Egyptian linen from a foreign land. This isn't necessarily bad. However, it does show that the harlot doesn't mind buying expensive things. The virtuous woman *makes* her own clothing and tapestry. Not only that, but she sells these items.

Note how her husband is an elder of the land, and is well known. One can't help but recall the phrase, "Behind every great man is a great woman."

Proverbs 31:25-27 says,

25. Strength and honor [are] her clothing; she shall rejoice in time to come.

26. She opens her mouth with wisdom, and on her tongue [is] the law of kindness. 27. She watches over the ways of her household, and does not eat the bread of idleness.

The woman of valor wears strength and honor. Also, joy is coming. However, not a fleeting joy. It is a meaningful, permanent joy. Verse 26 says that she speaks wisdom and kindness. She isn't cynical or mean-spirited. Remember a person's words reflect where their heart is (Luke 6:45). The virtuous woman watches over her household. She does this task with meticulous scrutiny and with a watchful eye. She looks over the actions of her children. She is busy; she isn't prone to idleness. Idleness often leads to idle talk and gossip.

Proverbs 31:28-31 says,

28. Her children rise up and call her blessed; her husband [also], and he praises her. 29. "Many daughters have done well, but you excel them all." 30. Charm [is] deceitful and beauty [is] passing, but a woman [who] fears the Lord, she shall be praised. 31. Give her of the fruit of her hands, and let her own works praise her in the gates.

Verse 29 is a quote. In other words, there is outside recognition of her excellence. She is superior to all other women. Her children and her husband call her blessed.

Verse 30, emphasizes the fleeting nature of outside beauty. In reference to an evil woman, Proverbs 9:17 says, *do not lust after her beauty in your heart, nor let her allure you with her eyelids.* It also points out the deceitfulness of a charming personality or physical beauty. When two people actually live together, any façades fade. The true nature eventually shows. Though beauty and charm fade away with time, a fear of the Lord never fades. It is a shame that even in the Church, beauty and charm trump the fear of the Lord.

Verses 10 to 31 of Proverbs 31 is called the *Eishes Chayil*. It is the praise of an ideal wife in Judaism. It is said to have been praise directed from the husband to the wife. Note that if Lemuel is Solomon, then this advice is coming from Bathsheba. Bathsheba herself was the wife of a king (Beck). In the end, as verse 31 says, the woman of valor will get what she worked for. In the end, her works will praise her.

Chapter 14 – God is Love

Often times, you may see a sign saying *God is Love*. It may be on bumper stickers, on a Gospel tract or even at football games. The phrase is true; the verse can be found in 1 John 4:16. However, due to overuse, the depth and truth behind the verse has been lost.

There are many thoughts on the subject of love. One young man I interviewed said the Nickelodeon movie *Snow Day* defines love perfectly.

He even quoted the movie, saying, "Love isn't about fate and magic bracelets and destiny. It's about finding someone you can stand to be around for 10 minutes at a time."

It does sound nice. However, I kind of don't want to get my advice on love from a kid's movie.

"You can't put time on love," he continued. "It is never too soon to fall in love. You can't tell yourself not to love someone. The harder you try, the more you'll love someone."

You may laugh. And you may not openly say things like this young man. Nonetheless, you may have the same ideas on love as him. We are all influenced by the world's portrayal of love, whether we realize it or not. In fact, the world's view of love has already infected the people of God.

The Greatest Commandment

Love is listed as a first fruit of the Spirit in Galatians 5:22. Love is described in depth in 1 Corinthians 13. In this passage, Paul describes love as being greater than knowledge, prophecy, and faith. 1 Peter 4:8 says that love covers a multitude of sins; in other words, it is forgiving. Romans 8:31-39 goes in-depth describing that nothing can separate us from the love of Jesus Christ.

Matthew 22:35-40 says,

35. Then one of them, a lawyer, asked [Him a question], testing Him, and saying, 36. "Teacher, which [is] the great commandment in the law?" 37. Jesus said to him, " 'You shall love the Lord your God with all your heart, with all your soul, and with all your mind.' 38. This is [the] first and great commandment. 39. And [the] second [is] like it: 'You shall love your neighbor as yourself.' 40. On these two commandments hang all the Law and the Prophets."

Jesus just finished silencing several Sadducees concerning the topic of the resurrection. Then a lawyer came and tested him concerning the Law.

Jesus said, as written in verse 37, that the greatest commandment is to love the Lord with all your heart, soul and mind. Already you can see that love is intertwined with devotion. Those who tested Jesus may have had external expressions of love, such as keeping the

Sabbath. Nevertheless, they lacked the internal love to God. They did not love God with their heart, soul and mind.

So what does loving God have to do with loving your spouse, or potential mate? We will get to that soon enough. For this passage, let's keep it in the context of loving your neighbor.

Verse 39 says that the second commandment is like or related to the first. We are commanded to love our neighbors as we love ourselves. Our neighbor refers to everyone we come in contact with: friends, acquaintances, and people we just run into at the store.

In Verse 40, Jesus gives a concluding declaration. All the Law and the Prophets hang on these two commandments of love. In other words, if we keep the commandment to love God with our all (and others as ourselves), everything else will fall into place. We will treat our friends right. We will seek a mate in a way that glorifies God. We will love our spouse right.

The Law and the Prophets hang on love. That's practically the entire Old Testament. So the laws given to Israel, the prophecies concerning the Coming of Messiah, and everything else rests on love. And this is not just a shallow, flimsy love; instead, this is a deep love. This is a sacrificial love.

In order to have a better understanding of love, we must look to the very personification of love: the Lord God. If we, the Church of God, had a better understanding of God's love for us, we wouldn't be searching for all these false loves in the world.

Love Bestowed causes Obedience

An intellectual understanding of God's love isn't enough. We must ask the Lord to take us deeper.

1 John 3:1-3 says,

1. Behold what manner of love the Father has bestowed on us, that we should be called children of God! Therefore the world does not know us, because it did not know Him. 2. Beloved, now we are children of God; and it has not yet been revealed what we shall be, but we know that when He is revealed, we shall be like Him, for we shall see Him as He is. 3. And everyone who has this hope in Him purifies himself, just as He is pure.

John starts with a declaration: what matter of love has the Father bestowed on us that we should be called the children of God? Truly this is a miraculous thing: to be called the child of the One who created the universe.

Nevertheless, there is a consequence to being a child of God; the world will not know or love the Christian. Jesus said if they hated me, they would hate you (John 15:18-27). This hatred is more unconscious than it is conscious. When a lost person repents and places faith in Jesus, only then is that hatred turned to a love for God. This is why Jesus is our first love (Revelation 2:4). We never knew the love of God before we knew Him.

1 John 3:4-8 says,

4. Whoever commits sin also commits lawlessness, and sin is lawlessness. 5. And you know that He was manifested to take away our sins, and in Him there is no sin. 6. Whoever abides in Him does not sin. Whoever sins has neither seen Him nor known Him. 7. Little children, let no one deceive you. He who practices righteousness is righteous, just as He is righteous. 8. He who sins is of the devil, for the devil has sinned from the beginning. For this purpose the Son of God was manifested, that He might destroy the works of the devil.

John writes that those who have love bestowed on them from God are obedient to God. Disobedience is preferred, even among believers at times. However, love bestowed or salvation from eternal damnation causes obedience.

Why is it written *let no man deceive you*? Because many say obedience to God is not required, either explicitly or implicitly. Yet, obedience to the Lord is a sign of true love for God.

Obviously we all make mistakes. Though, the sin John speaks of here is continual, habitual sin. This denotes a practice of sin, as Jesus spoke of in (Matthew 7:23).

Love grounds and roots the believer. Ephesians 3:17 says, *that Christ may dwell in your hearts through faith; that you, being rooted and grounded in love.* Have you ever doubted someone's love for you? Your parents? Your friends? Maybe your love interest? It isn't a pleasant feeling.

Have you ever doubted God's love for you? I know I have. It creates instability, insecurity and unsteadiness. Then when I sit with God, in prayer or reading the Word, I am reassured of His love. I am reminded that His love is faithful to the end; stability returns.

Having faith in God's love creates a grounded heart. Note how communication is the key factor. Prayer is a two-way street of communication with God. We speak to God, and God speaks to our heart. Compare stability to limerence and infatuation. Joshua Harris writes about how love is normally portrayed in the world as *being out of our control*. People are said to be "madly in love." Also, people are said to be "falling in love." In other words, it is in our language.

"Why do we feel compelled to compare love to a pit or a mental disorder?" Joshua Harris said. "What do these statements reveal about our attitudes toward love? I think part of the reason we make these somewhat overstated analogies is because they remove responsibility. If a person falls into a pit, what can she do about it (Harris)?"

1 John 3:9-12 says,

9. Whoever has been born of God does not sin, for His seed remains in him; and he cannot sin, because he has been born of God. 10. In this the children of God and the children of the devil are manifest: Whoever does not practice righteousness is not of God, nor [is] he who does not love his brother. 11. For this is the message that you heard from the beginning, that we should love one another, 12. not as Cain [who] was of the wicked one and murdered his brother. And why did he murder him? Because his works were evil and his brother's righteous.

Even the ultimate sacrifice of Jesus Christ shows the ultimate form of obedience. Jesus was obedient to the Father unto death. As a result, those who are saved are *manifest* or obvious. They practice righteousness.

Love restricts us and causes us to be dead to sin. Because of the love we have for God, we no longer love the world and its delights. By love, we judge that we are new creatures in Christ (2 Corinthians 5:17).

Unbelievers are also made manifest by their works of disobedience (this includes Christians whose actions don't line up with their words). Those who are disobedient do not know what kind of love the Father has bestowed. Christians are marked also in that they love each other. Note that this love isn't to be confused with enablement. If you truly love someone, you will, in meekness and humility, warn him or her if they are doing something wrong.

If the World Hates You...

Unfortunately, the world doesn't always understand true love. It fact, it hates it. 1 John 3:13-16 says,

13. Do not marvel, my brethren, if the world hates you. 14. We know that

we have passed from death to life, because we love the brethren. He who does not love [his] brother abides in death. 15. Whoever hates his brother is a murderer, and you know that no murderer has eternal life abiding in him. 16. By this we know love, because He laid down His life for us. And we also ought to lay down [our] lives for the brethren.

Christians are told to not marvel if the world hates them. Note this is relational: they hate us because they hate God. Note that if a Christian hates his brother something is direly wrong.

In verse 14, loving the brethren proves true salvation and true love from the Father. This is connected with enjoying fellowship with other believers and not necessarily with unbelievers. If a Christian doesn't like being with the Body of Christ, something is wrong. In the sight of God, a hateful thought is just as bad as an action (Matthew 5:22). Whoever hates his brother is called a murderer in verse 15. For example, enablement is a form of hatred.

This also defines the conflict within missionary dating. How can the Christian get involved with a lost person, who spiritually hates God? This hate may not be conscious. But in terms of biblical Christianity, any unregenerate mind hates God.

Verse 16 says that we know love because Jesus laid down His life for us. As a result, we ought to lay down our lives for the brethren. Therefore, sacrifice for others is a sign of true love.

1 John 3:17-19 says,

17. But whoever has this world's goods, and sees his brother in need, and shuts up his heart from him, how does the love of God abide in him? 18. My little children, let us not love in word or in tongue, but in deed and in truth. 19. And by this we know that we are of the truth, and shall assure our hearts before Him.

Providing for a brother's need is a sign of the love of God in a person. Note how John uses providing for a brother's need. This is related to what Jesus said about provision for the brethren (Matthew 25:44). The lost are not His; Jesus doesn't even know the lost. There is nothing wrong with feeding the poor or helping out the community. However, the text refers to believers providing for the needs of believers.

Verse 19 shows how love is not just spoken with words, but actual deeds. Consequently, with deeds, the love of God is shown to be true in the believer. Also, performing deeds assures the heart before the Lord. In other words, our works prove our love for God, just as our works prove our faith in God.

1 John 3:20-24 says,

20. For if our heart condemns us, God is greater than our heart, and knows all things. 21. Beloved, if our heart does not condemn us, we have confidence toward God. 22. And whatever we ask we receive from Him, because we keep His commandments and do those things that are pleasing in His sight. 23. And this is His commandment: that we should believe on the name of His Son Jesus Christ and love one another, as He gave us commandment. 24. Now he who keeps His commandments abides in Him, and He in him. And by this we know that He abides in us, by the Spirit whom He has given us.

Verse 20 says our hearts can condemn us if our works do not reflect our profession of loving God. Verse 22 emphasizes again the need to keep His commandments. Because of our obedience, we ask and receive, according to His will.

A Love the World Knows Not

This love is intertwined with repentance and faith. Remember though, the world does not comprehend this love. 1 John 4:1-3 says,

1. Beloved, do not believe every spirit, but test the spirits, whether they are of God; because many false prophets have gone out into the world. 2. By this you know the Spirit of God: every spirit that confesses that Jesus Christ has come in the flesh is of God, 3. and every spirit that does not confess that Jesus Christ has come in the flesh is not of God. And this is the spirit of the Antichrist, which you have heard was coming, and is now already in the world.

John tells us to not believe every doctrine or spirit. This is similar to how Paul tells believers to not be tossed around by every wind of doctrine (Ephesians 4:14). We are called to test the spirits. Anyone that says that God has not come in the flesh in the form of Jesus Christ is Antichrist or against Christ. It also means an alternative to Christ.

1 John 4:4-6 says,

4. You are of God, little children, and have overcome them, because He who is in you is greater than he who is in the world. 5. They are of the world. Therefore they speak [as] of the world, and the world hears them. 6. We are of God. He who knows God hears us; he who is not of God does not hear us. By this we know the spirit of truth and the spirit of error.

The Holy Spirit in us is greater than he who is in the world, the Devil. Again, you can see a separation between the world and Christians. Those that are of the world speak as if they are of the world. Those that are of God hear God, and know when He speaks (John 10:27).

1 John 4:7-11 says,

7. Beloved, let us love one another, for love is of God; and everyone who loves is born of God and knows God. 8. He who does not love does not know God, for God is love. 9. In this the love of God was manifested toward us, that God has sent His only begotten Son into the world, that we might live through Him. 10. In this is love, not that we loved God, but that He loved us and sent His Son [to be] the propitiation for our sins. 11. Beloved, if God so loved us, we also ought to love one another.

God Himself is love personified. How do we know the love of God? His love was manifested toward us by sending His Son the in flesh to dwell among men. Matthew says Jesus Christ is God with us (Matthew 1:23). What an amazing thought! For the Creator of the universe to actually come down to visit and save His creation!

Verse 10 reminds us that we were not searching for the Lord. Some may say they are trying to find Him. However, it is the Lord who finds us. He initiated the relationship while we were yet sinners (Romans 5:8).

He First Loved Us…

We will never fully comprehend God's love in this life. Even in the next life, I believe we will forever be learning the love of God.

1 John 4:12-15 says,

12. No one has seen God at any time. If we love one another, God abides in us, and His love has been perfected in us. 13. By this we know that we abide in Him, and He in us, because He has given us of His Spirit. 14. And we have seen and testify that the Father has sent the Son [as] Savior of the world. 15. Whoever confesses that Jesus is the Son of God, God abides in him, and he in God.

It is important to note that none have seen God at any time. Whereas loving an invisible God takes faith, loving a visible brother in Christ doesn't take as much faith. Love is perfected in us when we love unconditionally. Remember, Jesus asked His Father to forgive the Roman soldiers even as they were nailing Him to the Cross (Luke 23:34).

1 John 4:16-19 says,

16. And we have known and believed the love that God has for us. God is love, and he who abides in love abides in God, and God in him. 17. Love has been perfected among us in this: that we may have boldness in the day of judgment; because as He is, so are we in this world. 18. There is no fear in love; but perfect love casts out fear, because fear involves torment. But he who fears has not been made perfect in love. 19. We love Him because He first loved us.

Again, God is love. God and love abide in the true Christian. Verse 17 speaks of love being perfected in us for the Day of Judgment. I have heard various explanations as to what fear refers to in this passage. However, the reader must remember the context. The previous verse talks about boldness on the Day of Judgment. As a result, this is talking more of fear of judgment. Those who fear judgment have not been perfected in love or their relationship with God. This might mean that a fearful Christian might fear their salvation isn't secure by the love of God.

Insecurity of salvation could result from a lack of trusting in God's love. Interesting enough, this insecurity may result from a lack of obedience on the part of the Christian. In other words, disobedience produces uncertainty because the conscience is convicted. Verse 19 again focused the reader back on God's love for us.

1 John 4:20-21 says, *if someone says, "I love God," and hates his brother, he is a liar; for he who does not love his brother whom he has seen, how*

can he love God whom he has not seen? And this commandment we have from Him: that he who loves God [must] love his brother also.

Verse 12 is brought back to mind. If someone says they love God but hates their brother, it nullifies their words. For example, how can Christians say they love God, but run from fellowship? The task of loving a brother in Christ confirms love for the invisible Eternal God.

Forgiveness is a key aspect of love. Peter asked Jesus how many times a man ought to forgive his bother. Jesus replied seventy times seven times (Matthew 18:22). In other words, we need to lose track of how many times a person sins against us. We need to throw out the checklists.

Love covers all sins. Note how hate causes strife, as it does not forget sins, and keeps bringing them up. Jesus doesn't ignore sin. He recognizes them, and covers them with His blood.

What I have come to learn from all of the interviews and research is that we, as believers, need to love the Lord, with all of our heart, soul, and mind. From there, all of our other loves (friendships, dating, marriages) will fall into place.

Chapter 15 – Conclusion

As this book comes to an end, one statement becomes clear: we must trust the Lord for our relationships. Instead of trusting God, many Christians venture into the world. These Christians take matters into their own hands. Sadly, these actions reveal the compromised state of the heart.

The Bible is obviously not free of people taking matters into their own hands. We all do to some extent. Abraham's wife Sarah is a major example. The Lord promised she would bear a son, despite being past the age of childbearing. Sarah laughs at the idea, since it appears so unbelievable.

The Lord answers her doubt with, "*Why did Sarah laugh, saying, 'Shall I surely bear a child, since I am old?' Is anything too hard for the Lord* (Genesis 18:13,14)?"

Sarah denied her laugh. In essence, she denies the fact that she disbelieved. Not unlike today, Christians may deny that missionary dating (or any form of compromise) is disbelief; however, it is.

God is not ignorant of our needs. He is God. He knows what you need, before you even ask Him (Matthew 6:8). The Lord will make provision for His children.

Matthew 7:7-10 says,

7. "Ask, and it will be given to you; seek, and you will find; knock, and it will be opened to you. 8. For everyone who asks receives, and he who seeks finds, and to him who knocks it will be opened. 9. Or what man is there among you who, if his son asks for bread, will give him a stone? 10. Or if he asks for a fish, will he give him a serpent?

What if the comprised Christian says they have asked and have not received? Well is it possible they are asking for what they don't need? Is it possible they are asking for a stone, when their Father wants them to have bread?

Maybe we want to get into a relationship with the wrong person. And God, unwilling to have us make the wrong choice, keeps us from that. So we keep searching, when all we need to do is humble ourselves before the providence of God.

Matthew 7:11 says, *if you then, being evil, know how to give good gifts to your children, how much more will your Father who is in heaven give good things to those who ask Him!*

Note the verse says good gifts. Not bad gifts. The Father denies us, and in many cases, protects us of our ignorant desires. It is when God finally lets us wholly embrace the bad gifts that we need to be worried.

In a materialistic world, we want what we want and we want it now. Without Jesus, the desire for what we want restricts us. Without Jesus, we are literally blinded by what we see. Nevertheless, the Lord calls us to trust Him.

In our search for a mate, we must have faith. Not just faith that the Lord will send someone, but also faith to do what is right. Hebrews 11:1 says *faith is the substance of things hoped for, the evidence of things not seen.*

I heard it said that singles pray for a mate, while married people pray for the Rapture. It is always greener on the other side. In an increasingly compromised church, finding another saved individual seems hopeless. However, the Lord is faithful.

Prayer, as in any situation, is crucial. I wrote this *Guide* initially for Christian singles considering dating lost individuals. During the writing of the third draft, I was single. I know, during my singlehood, prayer for a wife was one of my requests. However, I prayed even more for the Lord to *prepare* me during this state to be a godly husband and father.

Someone Should Write A Book…

I remember when I first told Pastor Jay Peters about the *Guide*. This was years ago. We were eating Chinese food for lunch, and talked about many things. I asked him if he knew of any Christians who got into a relationship with a lost person, and what were the results.

Pastor Jay struggled with the sheer number of relationships. He briefly went over a few couples, and stated that someone should write a book about that. By that point, I had already started gathering notes on the subject. I then informed Jay of my new project, the Proverbs' Guide.

Love is something we seek and something we hope for. However, what kind of love we seek is questionable. In addition, are we willing to love like Jesus? I pray that I can love someone unconditionally. It is a hard thing to write, and I know I can only do it with God's strength.

Some Christians think that once they find that soul mate, everything will be perfect. They place all their happiness on that one person, who is flawed. The truth is that you can't find happiness in another broken person.

Maybe you are reading this book, and you are not a Christian. A lot of the material in this book may sound like nonsense.

The only way to discern the things of the Spirit is with the Spirit (1 Corinthians 2:14). Paul says in the same verse that spiritual things are foolishness to those without the Spirit. I would like to invite any nonbeliever reading this book to a personal relationship with Jesus Christ. 2000 years ago, God came down to earth as the Man, Jesus Christ (John 1:1,14). Jesus was crucified, died, and rose again on the third day (1 Corinthians 15:1-4). Isaiah 53:5 says, *He [was] wounded for our transgressions, [He was] bruised for our iniquities; the chastisement for our peace [was] upon Him, and by His stripes we are healed.* On the Cross, Jesus took the punishment we rightful deserved.

Place your faith in Jesus and the blood He spilled for your sins (Ephesians 2:8-9). Repent of (or turn away from) your sins against God (Luke 13:2). Ask the Lord to forgive you of your sins. Romans 10:13 says, *whoever calls on the name of the Lord shall be saved.* If you pray this in truth, the Spirit will abide in you (1 Corinthians 6:19-20) and guide you (John 16:13). Jesus will not fail you.

Maybe you are a Christian, but you made some serious mistakes. Perhaps you married someone you missionary dated and your spouse is still lost. There is hope for those who got into such relationships. 1 John 1:9 says, *if we confess our sins, He is faithful and just to forgive us [our] sins and to cleanse us from all unrighteousness.*

Even if we failed, the Lord is willing to pick us up again. It may be tough to stay in an unequally yoked marriage, but the Lord will honor it. Humble yourself and recommit your ways to Christ. Psalms 51:17 says that the Lord will not despise a broken and contrite heart.

And this leads us back to the starting point of this book: a saved individual dating a lost person. I still don't approve, as the Bible is against it, as well as the obvious consequences.

In the end, we must ask the Lord to remove ungodly desire from all our hearts, and replace it with sacrificial love. Thank you for reading and God Bless.

References

All Scripture is from the New King James Bible (NKJV) © 1984 by Thomas Nelson, Inc.

Chapter 3

Smith, Chuck. "2 Corinthians 6." <u>The Word for Today</u>. Blue Letter Bible. 1 Jun. 2005. Retrieved 10 Aug. 2009. <www.blueletterbible.org>

Chapter 4

Tennov, Dorothy. <u>Love and Limerence: The Experience of Being in Love</u>. Lanham: Scarborough House, 1979, 1999.

Chapter 5

Henry, Matthew. "Commentary on Hosea 4." Blue Letter Bible. 1 Mar. 1996. Retrieved 10 Aug. 2009. <www.blueletterbible.org>

Cook, Paul. "Soul Tie." Porn-Free. 10 Aug. 2009. <www.porn-free.org>

Thompson, D.D. Ph.D, Frank Charles. Thompson Chain-Reference Bible (King James Version). Indianapolis: B.B. Kirkbride Bible Co., Inc, 1988. p. 1607

Slick, Matt. "What is the biblical purpose of sex?" Christian Apologetics & Research Ministry. 20 Aug. 2009. <www.carm.org>

Chapter 7

Ropelato, Jerry. "Internet Pornography Statistics 2009." TopTenREVIEWS. 20 Aug. 2009. <www.toptenreviews.com>

Strabo. Geography VIII.vi.20

Thompson, D.D. Ph.D, Frank Charles. Thompson Chain-Reference Bible (King James Version). Indianapolis: B.B. Kirkbride Bible Co., Inc, 1988. p. 1621

Chapter 8

Athanasius. History of the Arians. 278

Cook, Paul "Being Single." Porn-Free. 23 Sep. 2009. <www.porn-free.org>

Grace, Rebecca. "Singles, sex and the Christian community." AFA Journal. Aug. 2009. p. 12. <www.afajournal.org> *Note: Grace has married since the publication of this article, and her name is now Rebecca Grace Davis.*

Chapter 9

Croft, Scott. Sex and the Supremacy of Christ. Wheaton: Crossway (Good News Publishers), 2005. p. 145-149. <www.crossway.org>

Harris, Joshua. I Kissed Dating Goodbye. Colorado Springs: Multnomah Books, 2003. p. 188

Chapter 11

Grace, Rebecca. "Messy marriages in the hands of a gracious God." AFA Journal. Feb. 2009. p. 21. <www.afajournal.org>

Ricucci, Gary and Betsy. Love that Lasts: Making a Magnificent Marriage. Gaithersburg: People of Destiny, 1992.

Chapter 12

Sratling. Cassandra. "Blended families can overcome daunting odds." Detroit Free Press. 9 Jun. 2009.

Chapter 13

Beck, Shari. The Proverbs Principle.

Chapter 14

Harris, Joshua. <u>I Kissed Dating Goodbye</u>. Colorado Springs: Multnomah Books, 2003. p. 66

About the Author

Armand J. Azamar is a freelance writer, illustrator and the founder of Broken Owl Productions. He was born again (became a Christian) in May 2001. Azamar has written for various publications, including *Geeks Under Grace*, *Altered Reality*, and *Live*. Azamar received his Bachelor's Degree in Communications at Governors State University, May 2014. He is also a teacher at New Life Assembly Church (www.nlachurch.com).

www.ingramcontent.com/pod-product-compliance
Lightning Source LLC
Chambersburg PA
CBHW060536100426
42743CB00009B/1542